The Woman

of

Wonder

THE BATTLE CRY
CHRISTIAN MINISTRIES

PASTOR (MRS.) SHADE OLUKOYA

The Woman Of Wonder

Shade Olukoya

© July 2010 - THE WOMAN OF WONDER
SHADE OLUKOYA

ISBN-13: 978-0692276587

THE BATTLE CRY CHRISTIAN MINISTRIES
322, Herbert Macaulay Way, Sabo, Yaba,
P. O. Box 12272,
Ikeja, Lagos.

Phone: 08033044239 - 018044415

All Scripture is from the King James Version.

Cover illustration by: Sister Shade Olukoya

DEDICATION

Dedicated to the Mountain of Fire and Miracles
Ministries Women Foundation

Chapter

1

·A
Prophetic
Message

*For I know the thoughts that I think
towards you, saith the LORD, thoughts of
peace, and not of evil, to give you an
expected end. Jer. 29:11*

G od has a unique message for this generation. The agenda of the Almighty is so unique that we have to tighten up our belts and re-address certain issues. God is the creator of the entire universe. His purpose may not be known to us, but He has a purpose.

> *For I know the thoughts that I think toward you, saith the LORD, thoughts of peace and not of evil, to give you an expected end.* Jeremiah 29:11

"Behind every successful man is a woman." This statement has become a trite in our generation, but if you take a second look at the statement, you will discover that women are the shakers and movers of the society. The society may not accord positions of prominence to women, but recent global issues are making people all over the world to come to grips with the fact that women can no longer be cast aside.

WOMEN AND NATION BUILDING

The world needs to wake up to acknowledge the role of women in nation building. The Church too needs to wake up and rediscover the invaluable role of women in the Church. The truth is that, God has used several women to play salient and important roles. God has used women like Mother Florence Crawford as the founder of the Apostolic Faith. God has used Amiee Semple McPherson as the founder of the International Four Square Gospel Church. Even when women have not been directly used as founders of global ministries, women have played important roles in various Church revivals across the globe.

6

We will need to take a second look at the role of women for a number of reasons. While it is true that God has used women marvellously, it is equally true that the devil has borrowed women and used them as evil vessels. It is crystal clear that women play important roles either for good or for evil. Right from the beginning of creation, God has accorded a position of prominence to women; hence He created mankind male and female.

> *And he answered and said unto them, Have ye not read, that he which made them at the beginning made them male and female,* Matthew 19:4

> *And the LORD God said, It is not good that the man should be alone; I will make him an help meet for him.* Genesis 2:18

THE AGENDA

The purpose of God for the world requires contribution and involvement of both male and female genders. Hence, either in the political realm or in the Church, we have witnessed the direct involvement of women. Christianity has grown in Africa by leaps and bounds. Even in the Mountain of Fire and Miracles Ministries, we have witnessed the involvement of women for some two decades. As we take a cursory look at the progress God has allowed M.F.M.M. women to make, we have had to cast our minds back to God's prophetic covenant given to us at the inception of this ministry.

7

One thing that is prominent is that, we must release the destinies of women in order to allow them fulfil their roles, as God continues to unfold His agenda for Mountain of Fire and Miracles Ministers. The promises of God for women who would yield themselves as willing instruments are so great that we may not be able to put them all on the pages of this book. However, one thing is clear; the future of our women is indeed great and glorious. God is ready to anoint our women with power to do exploit. God is going to use our female members to make a lot of impact on the society. Our women who are in business are going to be the richest and the most successful.

The prophetic agenda of God is indeed wonderful. Women who have served the Lord sincerely these two decades are going to be rewarded. Female ministers and leaders are going to take the gospel far and wide. What God is set to do is awesome. We must therefore allow Him to show us true revelations from His word. The contents of this book are for all and sundry. You do not have to be a woman to benefit from it.

Every reader has a mother, an aunt, a sister, a daughter, or a female colleague at work. We must join our hands together in order to allow God to fulfil His agenda for this end-time. In my travels locally and internationally, I have been challenged by the passion, the commitment, the energy, the drive and the joy manifested by the womenfolk. Our programmes locally and internationally have validated the fact that women have a critical role to play in God's end-time programme.

8

As we examine this topic, let us clear certain misconceptions concerning women:

1. **Women are not inferior-** We should not see women as people who play second roles and no more. It is wrong for you as a woman to go about with inferiority complex. It does not augur well for women to conclude that they are so inferior that they are not to be seen or heard.

As far as God's agenda is concerned, women are going to do exploit. Soon, women will be raised up to carry out global healing ministries, just as God has used men in many lands. When God anoints a woman, there is nothing like inferiority complex.

2. **Women are not evil, either in the Church or in the society-** Negative opinions have been flying here and there that; "Women are evil." God has given women to families, communities and nations to act as angels. We should do away with any negative mind-set and see women as people who have been created by God to contribute positively wherever they are found.

3. **Women are not agents of the devil-** The belief in some quarters is that women are mostly agents of darkness. This is not so! Women are capable of manifesting angelic virtues. The dark side of some women should not be used to cast aspersions on all women.

4.   **Women are not fond of pulling down their spouses or male colleagues-** Women are builders, not caterpillars. If women are given a chance to function in any capacity, they could play constructive and supportive roles in a powerful way. Most of the time, women are busy working behind the scene and building men up. It is just that the complementary roles of women are yet to be recognised.

5.   **Women are not useless-** They are useful. People often opine that women are passive wherever they are found. This too is not true. Women can be as active as their male counterparts. If you study women, you will discover that they can do as much good in the society as men. When God created the woman, it was the turn of Adam to pass commentary on the woman.

> *And Adam gave names to all cattle, and to the fowl of the air, and to every beast of the field; but for Adam there was not found an help meet for him. And the LORD God caused a deep sleep to fall upon Adam and he slept: and he took one of his ribs, and closed up the flesh instead thereof; And the rib; which the LORD God had taken from man, made he a woman, and brought her unto the man. And Adam said, This is now bone of my bones, and flesh of my flesh: she*

shall be called Woman, because she was taken out of Man. Therefore shall a man leave his father and his mother, and shall cleave unto his wife: and they shall be one flesh. Genesis 2:20-24

According to the original Greek interpretation when Adam said; "And she shall be called woman", he simply meant that she shall be called the man with a womb. This shows that women have characteristics of men but they have an added advantage of having a womb which men do not have. This shows that a woman is a creature of God who has an added advantage of being able to do something a man cannot do. What a wonder!

PRAYER POINTS

Behold, I will make them of the synagogue of Satan, which say they are Jews, and are not, but do lie; behold, I will make them to come and worship before thy feet, and to know that I have loved thee. Revelation 3:9

1. Holy Spirit, multiply Your grace upon my life, in the name of Jesus.

2. Anointing of revelation, fall upon my spirit man, in the name of Jesus.

3. Anointing of wisdom, fall upon my inner man, in the name of Jesus.

4.   Holy Ghost Fire, open the eyes of my spirit, in the name of Jesus.

5.   O Lord, let all the angels assigned to assist me, receive fire, in the name of Jesus.

6.   Any power that has arrested my angels, release my angels and be arrested, in the name of Jesus.

7.   O mighty hand of God, fall upon me for ministry and protection, in the name of Jesus.

8.   O Lord, let my descendants and I dwell under the shadow of the Almighty, all the days of our lives, in the name of Jesus.

9.   .O Lord, keep my family, my descendants after me and I in Your pavilion, in the name of Jesus- for in your pavilion, evil arrows cannot locate us.

10.   Evil arrows that came into my life by night, jump out and come out of my life by fire! in the name of Jesus.

11.   O Lord God of Elijah, arise in Your power, and let all my enemies fall before me, in the name of Jesus.

12.   O Lord, whenever my enemies plan any attack against me in the future, let their counsel fall into foolishness, in the name of Jesus.

13. O Lord, whenever my enemies take evil decision against me, let Your truth deliver me according to Thy Word, in the name of Jesus. *(Pray for those who are victims of the false accusations and slander from brethren in the house of God).*

NOTES:

_____

_____

_____

_____

_____

_____

_____

_____

_____

_____

_____

_____

_____

_____

_____

_____

_____

_____

_____

_____

_____

_____

_____

_____

Chapter

2

The
Cradle
and the
Kitchen

*And he answered and said unto them,
Have you not read, that he which made
them at the beginning made them male
and female, Matt 19:4*

At this point, let us take a look at the two critical reasons why women are important. These two areas portray the fact that women cannot be dismissed with a wave of the hand.

1.   **The cradle-** Every life begins at the cradle. The richest man, the greatest scientist, the most popular politician and the most celebrated V.I.P. all started at the cradle. No wonder it is said that, "The hand that rocks the cradle rules the world." If women do not play their roles well at the cradle, the world would be robbed of stars, philanthropists, inventors, sportsmen and women, political leaders, etc. The cradle is the place where virtues of women come to the fore.

At the cradle, the patience, the perseverance, the longsuffering, the care, the compassion, and the astuteness of women are visible. At the cradle, women go through sleepless nights, carry out dirty functions like cleaning the mess and washing diapers, just to keep babies comfortable and healthy. At the cradle, mothers display unusual intuition when they are able to spot what is wrong with babies who are not able to talk.

It is the mother who keeps feeding and watching over the child during moments of sickness, teething and children's adaptation to climatic changes. It is the mother who rocks the baby to sleep when the baby struggles to catch a sleep. The cradle offers the mother an opportunity to display her rare skills. Most of the time, we hardly link the cradle with moments of greatness in life, but the cradle is the beginning of greatness and the people you find at the cradle are mostly mothers.

2.   **The kitchen-** People have humorously stated that
the kitchen is the woman's office; however, it is much
more than that. The kitchen is a place of service. It
is a place where women labour with a servant's
heart. Most of the time, men love good food, but
they are busy pursuing business or career and as
such, they do not have time for the kitchen. It is the
mother, the wife and the home maker who knows
how to purchase groceries; prepare home made
salad; cook healthy and medicinal vegetables and
feed the entire family in a way that will make
everybody healthy.

The best moment in the home is when mummy comes out of
the kitchen with a smile, and with delicious food for the
entire family. Often times, mum must have spent close to
two hours or more mixing vegetables and ingredients
together, cooking yam and pounding it. Of course she
would wipe off sweat intermittently, but her joy is to make the
heart of every family member glad when they gather
together for breakfast, lunch or supper. The kitchen gives
the godly woman an opportunity to try healthy culinary skills
as she knows that family members cherish moments of
togetherness at meal times.

> *She riseth also while it is yet night, and*
> *giveth meat to her household, and a*
> *portion to her maidens.* Proverbs 31:15

It is interesting to know that Africans are very excited at
meal times. Men especially look forward to being served
good food by their wives. There are testimonies of broken
homes that God re-united when the wife decided to look

away from points of conflicts and satisfy the husband's craving for good food.

Most women have mistakenly underestimated the importance of the kitchen. A lot of women have lost their homes by paying little or no attention to their kitchens, but the truth of the matter is that, "The way to a man's heart is through his stomach." Even during times of hostility, women can build bridges by converting their kitchens to drawing boards and bringing out wonderful dishes. Even when the husband comes home frowning, he would put up a smile after devouring the content of a good dish.

THE KITCHEN AS A WEAPON

There is a story in the Bible which we need to examine. There was a serious war between Israel and an enemy nation. The captain of the forces of the enemy, Sisera, was captured by the wife of Heber the Canaanite. God pronounced blessings upon her because she succeeded in capturing an army general through her kitchen.

She had neither a gun nor any other weapon of warfare. Instead, her kitchen became her weapon of victory.

Let us read how she did it.

> *Blessed above women shall Jael the wife of Heber the Kenite be, blessed shall she be above women in the tent. He asked water, and she gave him milk; she brought forth butter in a lordly dish. She put her hand to the nail, and her right hand to the workmen's hammer; and with*

18

> *the hammer she smote Sisera, she smote*
> *off his head, when she had pierced and*
> *stricken through his temples. At her feet*
> *he bowed, he fell, he lay down: at her feet*
> *he bowed, he fell: where he bowed, there*
> *he fell down dead.* Judges 5:24-27

How powerful can a woman's kitchen be? Extremely powerful! Sisera had fought gallantly, and he was fagged out because the power of God from the heavenlies had battled him to exhaustion.

> *They fought from heaven; the stars in*
> *their courses fought against Sisera.*
> Judges 5:20

God needed someone to finish him off. Sisera merely asked for water, probably because he was extremely thirsty. How come he did not know that he was asking for water from an enemy? Only God knows the answer. Jael did not go into an argument, she did not abuse Sisera, her strength was in her kitchen.

She brought out milk and butter in an exotic casserole and as soon as Sisera saw what the woman brought out from her kitchen, he became a baby. Before Sisera knew what was happening, a woman had slain him. The secrets of her singular feat can only be traced to what she brought out of her kitchen.

As a woman, what type of delicacy do you bring out of your kitchen? Do you know that you can achieve with a good meal prepared from your kitchen what hours of arguments

19

cannot accomplish? The beauty of what Jael the wife of Heber did can only be traced to the fact that she must have cultivated the habit of making her kitchen an asset. She was not in the best of circumstances, but being a good woman, she was ever ready to bring out the best from her kitchen. When she was getting the milk and butter ready, she did not know that it would become an instrument of dealing with the enemy of God.

Jael could not fight on the battle field but she was a warrior in her kitchen. Wise women have cultivated the habit of praying while they cook. Do you know that no matter how tough your husband may be, you can pray over an excellent dish and offer it with common courtesy and submission? God will surely use the meal as a point of contact to accomplish what He has earmarked for your home.

Women who are wise will never think of punishing their husbands by starving them. Even if something is amiss between you and your husband, do not take the domestic conflict to the kitchen. Is there any squabble between you and your husband? The best way to settle it is to fix his best meal, and this will put paid to the squabble. The Biblical recipe has remained the same.

> *Therefore if thine enemy hunger, feed him; if he thirst, give him drink: for in so doing thou shalt heap coals of fire on his head.* Romans 12:20

Jael the wife of Heber lived during the era of the Old Testament, but she knew the principle enunciated in the passage above. Sisera her enemy was thirsty, she

20

prepared more than what he asked for, and that was the instrument of heaping coals of fire on Sisera. She did not give Sisera fire for fire, rather, she used a different method.

MILK AND BUTTER

Just imagine this scenario- There is a problem between a couple, the husband had become angry and if the wife too should give vent to anger, problems will erupt in the family. In some cases, a little quarrel had been compounded by the wife's reaction. Rather than invoke fire on the anxious nerves of Sisera, Jael a wise woman, came with milk and butter which ended any form of hostility. She could easily have said, "Why should I give you water, you don't deserve any drink." Then things could have jumped from frying pan into fire.

It takes wisdom to capture an enemy without using physical weapons. Research has proved that of all genders, the female gender is the most endowed with winning wisdom. Women have been known to have won where men failed. The inner qualities of women and the fact that they have been richly endowed to have calming effect on men explain why women have the capacity to succeed in special areas. In the whole of Israel, God needed to use someone and the person God used was a woman who was busy fixing meals in her kitchen.

There are times when the best place to win a war is in the kitchen. For example, if your husband happened to have been captured by a strange woman, you can covert your kitchen to a battlefield and set your husband free through your anointed meals. Jael used her bare hands to capture a warlord. She used ordinary milk and butter to mesmerise a warmonger. She traversed between her kitchen and possibly the front of her family's apartment to finish off a man whom God wanted to kill. What a wonder!

PRAYER POINTS

1. O Lord, Man of War, destroy the teeth of all those the devil will use against me in Your sanctuary, in the name of Jesus.

2. O Lord, break me, and mould me for Your glory, in the name of Jesus.

3. Every synagogue of satan erected against me, fall down before me now, for I am the beloved of the Lord, in the name of Jesus.

4.. Anything in me that will allow the arrow of the enemy to prosper, be removed now! in the name of Jesus.

5. Every demonic alteration of my destiny, loose your hold upon my life and come out of my foundation, in the name of Jesus.

6. All powers behind demonic alteration of my destiny, die! in the name of Jesus.

7. Any power behind demonic alteration of my handwriting and virtues, die! in the name of Jesus.

8. Demonic marriage, loose your hold over my life and be purged. out of my foundation, in the name of Jesus.

9. Every strange child assigned to me in the dream, be roasted by fire! in the name of Jesus.

10. I command the fire of God to pursue all strange children and women assigned to me in the dream, in the name of Jesus.

11. Every evil laying on of hands, loose your hold over my life and be purged out of my foundation, in the name of Jesus.

12. Evil idols from my father's house, fight against the idols from my mother's house and destroy yourselves, in the name of Jesus.

13. Every idol in my city of birth, holding down my destiny, be roasted by fire! in the name of Jesus.

14. Every demonic authority attacking my life as a result of my past relationship with strange sexual partners, be roasted by fire! in the name of Jesus.

15. Every demon activated against me, go back to your owner, in the name of Jesus.

NOTES:

Chapter

3

Women
Who
Win

*And the LORD God said, It is not good
that the man should be alone; I will
make him an help meet for him. Gen 2:18*

Herein lies the mystery of divinity. God specialises in using weak instruments to win stubborn warfare. The Bible says;

> *Then he answered and spake unto me, saying, This is the word of the LORD unto Zerubbabel, saying, Not by might, nor by power, but by my spirit, saith the LORD of hosts.* Zechariah 4:6

> *I returned, and saw under the sun, that the race is not to the swift, nor the battle to the strong, neither yet bread to the wise, nor yet riches to men of understanding, nor yet favour to men of skill; but time and chance happeneth to them all.* Ecclesiastes 9:11

If there is anywhere the strength of the Almighty finds best expression, it is in the life of women who are regarded as the weaker vessels.

The word weaker vessel is loaded with very revealing connotations. While women are called weaker vessels, it does not mean that they are so weak that they cannot do anything meaningful. The word weaker vessel actually means being made more delicately than men and consequently, more tender. By making women to be weaker vessels, God in His wisdom is bringing out an interplay of weakness and strength.

Men who are stronger are expected to complement the comparative weakness of the womenfolk. God wants the men who are more endowed with physical strength to show respect to the weaker vessel. The woman is to be dealt with, with special kindness, since she is feebler than man. Consequently, she needs more delicate attention. Men should know that women are slightly weaker, so they need careful attention since they are co-heirs of the grace of God.

THE WINNING STREAK

The wife, although weak needs due respect, kind attention, and affectionate assistance. God has woven together two types of fabric because He wants the weaker and stronger to come out in a perfect blend. God expects the man to dwell with the woman according to knowledge. However, most men lack knowledge as far as the details of the constitution of an average woman is concerned.

When you have knowledge as a man, you can dwell with any woman even if her character is somewhat undesirable. A man who takes time to study his spouse will succeed in relating well with her, even when she appears somewhat difficult to handle. One mistake men generally make is that they handle women with extremely tough hands, but here, God has given us an eye opener. Women are weaker, hence they need to be handled with tenderness and they should not be despised. Rather, men should give honour to them knowing that they are weaker.

THE KEY OF TENDERNESS

The weakness not withstanding, men and women are co-heirs of the grace of God. Here is another mystery, as far as the grace of God is concerned, there is nothing like superiority. Men and women are co-beneficiaries. One thing that men should learn at this point is that their prayer

27

can be hindered if they are guilty of handling women in a wrong manner. Both the husband and the wife are termed vessels or part of the furniture of God's house. The bottom line is that women need to be understood.

The woman is not termed weak in reference to intellectual or moral abilities, but purely in term of physical strength. When a wise man wants to deal with a woman, tenderness is the watchword. Women need to be protected by men and because women are weaker vessels, they are subsequently subject to infirmities, contempt, insults and likely to be cheated. Therefore, husbands should contribute their wisdom, authority, strength and ability to comfort, celebrate, protect, preserve and build up the women.

CHRIST'S EXAMPLE

The husband and the wife can be likened to different parts of the body. The Bible commands that the stronger parts of the body are supposed to bestow honour on the weaker part.

> *And those members of the body, which we think to be less honourable, upon these we bestow more abundant honour; and our uncomely parts have more abundant comeliness.* 1Corinthians 12:23

Again, we can learn a lot of lessons from the way Christ loves the Church. Although the Church is the body of Christ, it is made up of members who have their personal weaknesses and areas of imperfection. Christ has used His glory to cover the imperfection of the Church.

28

> *Husbands, love your wives, even as*
> *Christ also loved the church, and gave*
> *himself for it;* Ephesians 5:25

The problem with most couples can be traced to the inability of the husbands to dwell with their partners with care, knowledge, and love. We must learn a lesson from the Lord Jesus. When there is imperfection in the Church, He comes with love and tenderness.

When a woman makes a little mistake, some men flare up with emotions and terrible anger. Whereas the Bible teaches husbands to love their wives, and not to be bitter towards them.

> *Husbands, love your wives, and be not*
> *bitter against them.* Colossians 3:19.

If only husbands can be gentle towards their wives, there would be no room for divorce. The mistake most men make is that they exercise courtesy and politeness at work but react violently to the slightest provocation at home. This is unfair!

Do not give in to bitterness. Let the law of kindness rule your comportment, communication, action and reaction towards women. The world will become a better place when women become submissive and men come up with attitudes that portray wise understanding of the nature of women.

PRAYER POINTS

1.   All demons and principalities assigned against me, be decommissioned! in the name of Jesus.

2.   Every evil voice, rising up against my glory, be silenced! in the name of Jesus.

3.   Holy Spirit of God, do something new in my life today, in the name of Jesus.

4.   O Lord, make me an instrument of revival in Your hand.

5.   I shake off powers of demotion in my life, in the name of Jesus.

6.   Thou serpent of demotion, release my glory! in the name of Jesus.

7.   O heaven, arise and release me from captivity, in the name of Jesus.

8.   I render the weapons of my enemies useless, in the name of Jesus.

9.   Every weakness of my ancestors, that the enemy is using against me, die! in the name of Jesus.

10.   Every satanic conspiracy to cage my destiny, scatter! in the name of Jesus.

11.   Satanic strategy to delay me in the valley of life, die! in the name of Jesus.

12.   Satanic wisdom limiting my greatness, die! in the name of Jesus.

13.   Satanic power in my place of birth, that is manipulating my destiny, die! in the name of Jesus.

14.   I refuse to enter into the grave the enemy has prepared for me, in the name of Jesus.

15.   I refuse to become the wish of my enemy, in the name of Jesus.

16.   Every voice of the enemy over my life, be silenced by the power in the blood of Jesus.

17.   Every evil arrow of the enemy, fashioned against my destiny, backfire in the name of Jesus.

18.   Let the camp of my enemies be baptized with confusion, in the name of Jesus.

NOTES:

Chapter

4

The

MINISTRY

of

Women

Nevertheless neither is the man without the woman, neither the woman without the man, in the Lord. 1 Cor 11:11

There are lots of perverted opinions as regard what women are and what they do in the society. In Jewish time, women were viewed as glorified slaves. In some other eras, it was believed that women were neither to be seen nor heard. Some people have gone to a point where they believe that women are devils. Some men have carried this type of negative opinion where they see women as the scourge of humanity too far.

These views contribute a far cry from the divine view point. God does not create evil. God in His goodness cannot give you a thorn in your flesh. We need to go back to the Bible and discover the divine blueprint behind the creation of women.

God did not create the woman to torment the man. He created women to meet important needs in the life of men.

> *And the LORD God said, It is not good that the man should be alone; I will make him an help meet for him. And out of the ground the LORD God formed every beast of the field, and every fowl of the air; and brought them unto Adam to see what he would call them: and whatsoever Adam called every living creature, that was the name thereof. And Adam gave names to all cattle, and to the fowl of the air, and to every beast of the field; but for Adam there was not found an help meet for him. And the LORD God caused a deep sleep to fall upon Adam, and he slept: and he took one of his ribs, and*

34

closed up the flesh instead thereof; And the rib, which the LORD God had taken from man, made he a woman, and brought her unto the man. And Adam said, This is now bone of my bones, and flesh of my flesh: she shall be called Woman, because she was taken out of Man. Therefore shall a man leave his father and his mother, and shall cleave unto his wife: and they shall be one flesh. Genesis 2:18-24

The woman was created for the following reasons:

1.   **The woman as helper-** No matter how strong a man is, he needs help. God knows man's deepest needs; hence He has provided the woman to meet these needs. Again, God knows that the man is incomplete without the woman.

        Nevertheless neither is the man without the woman, neither the woman without the man, in the Lord. 1Corinthians. 11:11

Since the man is incomplete without the woman, the woman is a God sent helper. She has been created to introduce fullness to the life of the man.

2.   **The woman is a strong fence-** God has created the woman to act as a strong fence, protecting the entire family. One meaning of the original word help meet is, 'a strong fence or solid protection.' God created women as solid protection for the family. In the real sense, women constitute a strong fence to the family. If you take a look at an average home, you will see

35

the woman as the protective shield of the home. Careful attention to details, wisdom that keeps the home away from predators, busy bodies and trouble makers are women's strong points. If you take a look at Proverbs 31, you will discover the quiet but powerful role of the women.

The heart of her husband doth safely trust in her, so that he shall have no need of spoil. She will do him good and not evil all the days of her life. Proverb 31:11-12

Women constitute confidence, assurance and safety for the home. Many careful women have prevented spoils, tragedies, and destruction from entering the home. God has used women as gates that barricade evil from penetrating. **(Please read the story of David, Nabal and Abigail in 1 Samuel 25:2-38).** The Bible tells us that the snow cannot affect her home as she has taken proper precautions as the strong fence.

She is not afraid of the snow for her household: for all her household are clothed with scarlet. Proverbs 31:21

3.   **The woman as someone to lean on-** No matter how strong or talented a man is, he needs someone to lean on. God declared that it is not good for man to be alone. So, He moved close to the heart, took out a rib and made the woman. All that God needed from the body of man was the bone, and the place from where the bone was removed is highly instructive

> *And the LORD God caused a deep sleep to fall upon Adam, and he slept: and he took one of his ribs, and closed up the flesh instead thereof; And the rib, which the LORD God had taken from man, made he a woman, and brought her unto the man. And Adam said, This is now bone of my bones, and flesh of my flesh: she shall be called Woman, because she was taken out of Man.* Genesis 2:21-23

God did not take a rib from the leg of man. Hence, man would have thought of trampling upon the woman. God did not take a rib from the head of the man. That would have probably made the woman to contest the position of headship with the man. He took the rib from a place near the heart. The essence is to make man to have a special place in his heart for the woman. This reminds us of the fact that God wants men to have tender feelings and compassion for the women.

4.   **A woman is not an afterthought-** The creation of a woman is an original intention from God. God did not create the woman because He forgot to do so at the beginning, rather, women were in God's mind even before the beginning of creation.

5.   **Women are made of the finest materials-** God created man and declared that everything He had made was very good.

> *And God saw every thing that he had made, and, behold, it was very good. And the evening and the morning were the sixth day.* Genesis 1:31

Since it is crystal clear that the end of a thing is better than the beginning of it, by the time God moulded and created man, He as it were, created the woman as an improvement over His previous creation. The creation of the woman gave God an opportunity to bring out something better and more glorious. Hence, if you take a look at women, you will discover that they are filled with quiet, unassuming potentials. The materials with which God created women was the finest and the best. Man was made from no previous material; he was made from crude soil. The woman on the other hand was made from a material that had received the breath of the Almighty.

> *And the LORD God formed man of the dust of the ground, and breathed into his nostrils the breath of life; and man became a living soul.* Genesis 2:7

God bringing the woman out of the man suggests that the material with which God made the woman was well crafted and complete. Hence, women generally portray thoroughness and completeness.

6. **Women will assume positions of prominence in the Church and in the world-** The beauty of God's agenda for the world is that what He started to do by bringing the Saviour into the world through the womenfolk, He will bring to an end by coming up with a season of women empowerment. The prophetic destiny of God for our generation cannot be witnessed until we enter a season of the prophetic liberation and involvement of women of all ages. Women will once again enter centre stage

and they shall begin to do exploit for God.

7. **Women are life givers-** The fact that women have womb has endowed the womenfolk with an uncommon quality. The womb of the woman gives life. Hence, God has established women as life givers.

8. **The positive contribution of women-** Women contribute meaningfully to the society. The ideal godly woman is a pillar, not a caterpillar. She is a builder, not a destroyer. She is a destiny moulder, not a destiny destroyer. Women are capable of moving into any situation and ushering peace into chaotic situations. A real godly woman can step into a situation where there is a complete breakdown of law and order and work steadily and slowly until there is a noticeable positive change.

9. **Women have knack for thoroughness, patience and careful attention to details-** The way women are created, they are the only gender that are capable of being meticulous and painstaking. While the man is always on the go, the woman settles down quietly to analyze the consequences of the actions taken. If you put together a committee of ten that is made of nine men and one woman, it is only the woman who will remind the group of the vital areas that appeared to be neglected. That is why in government circles, efforts are made to ensure that appointments and positions are spiced with women.

10. There are certain things that only women can do-
     In God's economy, there are some roles which only
     women can play. For example, God has made it that
     it is only women that will bring children into the world.
     Even when the Saviour came into the world, He
     came through the womb of a woman.

     For unto us a child is born, unto us a son is
     given: and the government shall be upon
     his shoulder: and his name shall be called
     Wonderful, Counsellor, The mighty God,
     The
     everlasting Father, The Prince of Peace.
     Isaiah 9:6

     Therefore the Lord himself shall give you
     a sign; Behold, a virgin shall conceive,
     and bear a son, and shall call his name
     Immanuel. Isaiah 7:14

If the Lord came through a woman, it is pure sacrilege and
abomination of the highest order for scientists to attempt
making a man to carry pregnancy and deliver a child. When
the natural order is inverted, the devil is trying to pervert
God's plan for humanity.

We must pray against children of the devil who are trying to
introduce demonic practices in order to lead people astray.
We must be watchful lest they begin to tell us that there is no
God anywhere and that if scientists can produce a baby
from nowhere, then God is nowhere and that the virgin birth
is a ruse. They will then begin to question the fundamentals
of our faith.

11.   **Women add feminine touch wherever they come into the scene-** As God would have it, women are endowed with a soft feminine touch that is capable of diffusing tension and adding positive colour to situations. Even in the family, when things appear dry or flat, the mother comes up with her own touch and the atmosphere changes positively. When a boss becomes somewhat harsh to staff members and a woman intervenes, there is calmness. Some companies generally employ women to function in their customer service department because; the soft tones of a woman can calm down the nerves of an angry costumer. We need to benefit from the invaluable role of women in the family, in the Church, in communities, and establishments.

12.   **Women have a prophetic agenda to fulfil-** Women are daughters of destiny, and as such, God has created women to fulfil an important role in life. In these end-times, there is a unique prophetic agenda to fulfil. This is an age when God will use women in a very dynamic way. God will raise women up to fulfil their destiny in Christ. One of these days, women will become shakers and movers of the society. God will make use of woman to usher His prophetic plan into the world. Women will be empowered to do exploit. These are days when women cannot be dismissed with a wave of the hand. Women will rise gallantly and move up to their high places in Christ. Women will snatch themselves away from the shackles of slavery and begin to rule and reign with Christ. Women will move away from their neglected positions and begin to

41

surprise everyone. Women will declare "Enough is enough" and surprise those who have written off the womenfolk. This is the season of upliftment for women. This is the era of women of wonders! Now is the day when women will come out of hiding and take up vanguard positions to the glory of God. This is the moment when women will build up their inner strength and prove to the whole world that they are products of divine glory. Through women all over the world, God will showcase His glory and demonstrate His power. Watch it, women of wonder are coming!

PRAYER POINTS

1. Let God arise, and let all His enemies in my life be scattered, in the name of Jesus.

2. By the power in the blood of Jesus, I claim victory over all the powers of my enemies, in the name of Jesus.

3. Every failure of my father's house, attacking my life, die! in the name of Jesus.

4. Every circle of problem in my foundation, die! in the name of Jesus.

5. Every manipulation of the evil powers of my father's house to lead me into error, die! in the name of Jesus.

6. Every evil spoken word, delaying my breakthroughs, scatter! in the name of Jesus.

7.   Every satanic sacrifice, carried out against my
       life, backfire! in the name of Jesus.

8.   Every arrow of darkness, fired into my life,
       backfire! in the name of Jesus.

9.   Evil altars in my foundation, attacking my life,
       catch fire! in the name of Jesus.

10.   Every yoke of failure in my life, break into
       pieces,! in the name of Jesus.

11.   Every satanic agent, stealing from my life, be
       exposed and disgraced, in the name of Jesus.

12.   Evil walls standing between me and my
       breakthroughs, collapse! in the name of Jesus.

13.   I refuse to die unfulfilled, in the name of Jesus.

14.   Every foundational backwardness of my father's
       house, attacking my life, die! in the name of
       Jesus.

15.   Every satanic curse issued against my
       breakthroughs, break by the power in the blood
       of Jesus.

16.   Evil sacrifice manipulating my fruitfulness,
       catch fire! in the name of Jesus.

17.   Satanic altar attacking my breakthroughs,
       receive the thunder of God and scatter! in the
       name of Jesus.

43

NOTES:

Chapter

5

The

Women

Of

Wonder

She riseth also while it is yet night,
And giveth meat to her household,
And a portion to her maidens.
Prov. 31: 15

45

f there is any group of people capable of maximizing potentials, it is the womenfolk. Women are loaded with potentials. The lives of women are filled with untapped resources. Proverbs 31 portrays the best a woman can be. It highlights the qualities of the ideal woman otherwise called the virtuous woman.

The words of king Lemuel, the prophecy that his mother taught him. What, my son? and what, the son of my womb? and what, the son of my vows? Give not thy strength unto women, nor thy ways to that which destroyeth kings. It is not for kings, O Lemuel, it is not for kings to drink wine; nor for princes strong drink: Lest they drink, and forget the law, and pervert the judgment of any of the afflicted. Give strong drink unto him that is ready to perish, and wine unto those that be of heavy hearts. Let him drink, and forget his poverty, and remember his misery no more. Open thy mouth for the dumb in the cause of all such as are appointed to destruction. Open thy mouth, judge righteously, and plead the cause of the poor and needy. Who can find a virtuous woman? for her price is far above rubies. The heart of her husband doth safely trust in her, so that he shall have no need of spoil. She will do him good and not evil all the days of her life. She seeketh wool, and flax, and worketh willingly with her hands. She is like the merchants' ships;

46

she bringeth her food from afar. She riseth also while it is yet night, and giveth meat to her household, and a portion to her maidens. She considereth a field, and buyeth it: with the fruit of her hands she planteth a vineyard. She girdeth her loins with strength, and strengtheneth her arms. She perceiveth that her merchandise is good: her candle goeth not out by night. She layeth her hands to the spindle, and her hands hold the distaff. She stretcheth out her hand to the poor; yea, she reacheth forth her hands to the needy. She is not afraid of the snow for her household: for all her household are clothed with scarlet. She maketh herself coverings of tapestry; her clothing is silk and purple. Her husband is known in the gates, when he sitteth among the elders of the land. She maketh fine linen, and selleth it; and delivereth girdles unto the merchant. Strength and honour are her clothing; and she shall rejoice in time to come. She openeth her mouth with wisdom; and in her tongue is the law of kindness. She looketh well to the ways of her household, and eateth not the bread of idleness. Her children arise up, and call her blessed; her husband also, and he praiseth her. Many daughters have done virtuously, but thou excellest them all. Favour is deceitful, and beauty is vain: but a woman that feareth the

47

LORD, she shall be praised. Give her of the fruit of her hands; and let her own works praise her in the gates. Proverbs 31

The Bible teaches us that such a woman is priceless; she is a jewel of inestimable value; she is a treasure that can hardly be quantified. Women can rise and become the best. Women can get to the top. Women are capable of showing us that there is nothing grace cannot do. Women constitute a group of people who can draw upon the grace of God.

As a woman, you can excel. You can maximise your potentials and be a pacesetter. God is looking for women who will stand out of the crowd and prove to the world that being a woman does not matter and that a woman can demonstrate the fullness of God's grace. As a woman, you can make a great difference in your family, your community and in the Church. The only way is to look into the mirror of God's word and develop qualities that will bring out the glory of God.

The points below give credence to the fact woman can be exceptional and that they can come up with outstanding achievements:

1. **Research has proved that men with good wives generally live longer-** There is nothing that promotes longevity like the good influence of a godly woman. A lot of men have died prematurely because the women whom they lived with converted their lives on earth to hell. As a woman, you must conduct your affairs in such a manner as

to prolong the life of your husband. When a woman nags, complains and murmurs, life can be made miserable for the man. May God make you a woman that will enable the longevity of your husband, in the name of Jesus.

May God make you a woman whose total influence will keep your husband healthy and peaceful, in the name of Jesus.

2.   **A man who hates his mother without a cause will surely hate his wife-** The relationship between a man and his mother will influence his relationship with his wife as it will be the same yardstick he would use for his spouse. If you carry the negative attitude you have towards your mother to your family, you may discover that it will remain a replay of what you did previously.

They say, "Charity begins at home", but it does not end there. What you did not stop at home may be carried sooner or later to your new family.

PRAYER POINTS

1.   Every evil personality, using the night to pollute my life, I cut off your head, in the name of Jesus.

2.   Any evil power, claiming right to my breakthroughs, fall down and die! in the name of Jesus.

3.   Any power from the pit of hell, killing my breakthroughs, be devoured by the Lion of Judah, in the name of Jesus.

4.   I release the blood of Jesus into my career, in the name of Jesus.

5.   Every spirit of the tail, tying me down in the valley of poverty, die! in the name of Jesus.

6.   Every foundational poverty of my father's house, my destiny is not your candidate, release me and die! in the name of Jesus.

7.   Every circle of hardship in my foundation, release me and die! in the name of Jesus.

8.   Every blockage working against my breakthroughs, scatter! in the name of Jesus.

9.   I withdraw my name from the book of failure, in the name of Jesus.

10. I withdraw my name from the book of poverty, in the name of Jesus.

11. Every evil power, discouraging my helper, lose your power! in the name of Jesus.

12. I refuse to be a beggar in the market of life, in the name of Jesus.

13. By fire, by thunder, I possess all my possession in the warehouse of satan, in the name of Jesus.

14. I arise and shine, in the name of Jesus.

15. Wherever I go, favour shall follow me, in the name of Jesus.

16. I shall never be rejected in my place of blessing, in the name of Jesus.

17. Every blockage, standing between me and my helper, collapse and scatter! in the name of Jesus.

NOTES:

Chapter
6

Tapping
Uncommon
Resources

*And those members of the body, which
we think to be less honourable, upon
these we bestow more abundant
honour; and our uncomely parts have
more abundant comeliness. 1Cor. 12:23*

Women are endowed with uncommon resources. They are resilient. Just as men are eager to increase their pace, women are endowed with the gift of resiliency. It takes this kind of quality in a woman to hold on even when others are giving up. Setbacks are common occurrences in life, but it takes a winner to convert a setback to a comeback. God generally prepares women through unique experiences for a future of perseverance and solid innate qualities.

While the man may entertain the thoughts of giving up, women will always say, "Let us hold on a little longer." However, we must not shy away from the fact that some women are fond of giving up too soon. It is a spiritual attack for anyone to give up at the point of experiencing a breakthrough. Many men and women have erroneously thrown in the towel on the eve of their celebration. Such an act leaves much to be desired.

NEVER GIVE UP!

Fanny Crosby was a blind woman, yet she composed powerful songs inspite of the fact that she was physically challenged. She is one of the most gifted poets. As a blind poet, she wrote 8,000 hymns. I want you to meditate on three of her hymns.

SAFE IN THE ARMS OF JESUS

Safe in the arms of Jesus, safe on His gentle breast,
There by His love o'ershaded, sweetly my soul shall rest,
Hark 'tis the voice of angels, borne in a song to me,
Over the fields of glory, over the jasper sea.

Chorus:
Safe in the arms of Jesus, safe on His gentle breast
There by His love o'ershaded, sweetly my soul shall rest.

Safe in the arms of Jesus, safe from corroding care
Safe from the world's temptations, sin cannot harm me there.
Free from the blight of sorrow, free from my doubts and fears;
Only a few more trials, only a few more tears!

Jesus, my heart's dear refuge, Jesus has died for me;
Firm on the Rock of Ages, ever my trust shall be.
Here let me wait with patience, wait till the night is over;
Wait till I see the morning break on the golden shore.

SOME DAY

Some day the silver cord will break
And I no more as now shall sing
But, O, the joy when I awake
Within the palace of the King
And I shall see Him face to face
And tell the story saved by grace.

Some day my earthly house will fall,
I cannot tell how soon 'twill be,
But this I know; my All in All
Has now a place in heaven for me.
And I shall see Him face to face
And tell the story saved by grace.

Some day, when fades the golden sun
Beneath the rosy-tinted West,

My blessed Lord will say, 'Well done!'
And I shall enter into rest
And I shall see him face to face
And tell the story saved by grace

Some day-till then I'll watch and wait,
My lamp all trimmed and burning bright,
Than when my Saviour opens the gate,
My soul to Him may take its flight.
And I shall see him face to face,
And tell the story saved by grace.

REDEEMED

Redeemed, how I love to proclaim it!
Redeemed by the blood of the lamb;
Redeemed through His infinite mercy,
His child and forever I am.

Redeemed, redeemed
Redeemed by the blood of the Lamb
Redeemed, redeemed
His child and forever I am.

Redeemed, and so happy in Jesus,
No language my rapture can tell;
I know that the light of His presence
With me doth continually dwell.

I think of my blessed Redeemed
I think of Him all the day long;
I sing, for I cannot be silent;
His love is the theme of my song.

I know there's crown that is waiting,
In yonder bright mansion for me,
And soon, with the spirits made perfect,
At home with the Lord I shall be.

Let me share here with you the story of Ali Hafed; a man who gave up, not knowing that he was sitting on a goldmine. Ali Hafed was the owner of a very large farm land. His farm occupied acres of land. Farming did not seem to produce much yield and as the years went by, he became dissatisfied. He concluded that he had wasted his life just sitting idly in the farm land without reaping a good harvest.

One day, he felt that he had had enough and offered to sell the whole farm land to any available buyer. Buyers came and he sold it to one of them for peanuts. He collected he money and undertook a journey in search of an El-do-rado; something that will give him joy, satisfaction and wealth. Little did he know that his fortunes were tied to the farmland he had abandoned and sold off.

The new owner quickly settled in and made up his mind that he would make the best out of the farmland he had purchased. Initially, the farm did not yield anything extraordinary, but the new owner decided that he would persevere. While relaxing in the farm office one day, an old sage sauntered in. The sage exchanged pleasantries with the farm owner and they soon got into a long conversation. From nowhere, the sage exclaimed; "Diamonds! These are Diamonds!"

JUST PEBBLES

All of a sudden, the farm owner remembered what had happened the previous day. He had taken a long walk around the streams at the farmland and had stumbled across little pebbles that caught his fancy. He picked up some of them in order to adorn his table as keepsakes. These were the same pebbles that the sage was starring at. The sage got up, picked the pebbles and said reassuringly; "Yes, these are diamonds! I know diamond when I see one. Where on earth did you get these?" The owner of the farm replied; "By the stream."

He volunteered to take the old sage to the spot and by the time they got there, they saw several sparkling pebbles. The sage insisted, "These are diamonds!" Curiosity overwhelmed the owner of the farm. Soon, experts were brought in to confirm the rare find. The verdict was simple. There were acres of diamond deposit underneath the soil of the farm land and that was why crops were not growing. That was how the owner abandoned farming and began to mine and sell diamonds that made him extremely rich. He became so rich that he attracted national attention.

BENEATH THE SURFACE

Meanwhile, the previous owner had gone on a journey without destination. Eventually, he became penniless and hungry and he died. What do we learn from this story? If he had persisted, he would have been the one to discover that he had a large deposit of diamonds in his farm. The fact that he did not persevere robbed him of something that would have left him with stupendous wealth for generations.

58

Another farm owner somewhere in South Africa grew restive and angry when he discovered that his crops were not going properly. So he became frustrated and sold his farm. The person who purchased the farmland decided to explore the services of soil experts to determine the kind of crops that will thrive on the farm. They discovered that beneath the surface level, there was a huge deposit of gold. That was how one of the largest gold mines was discovered. Again, the new owner abandoned farming and settled down to a lifetime of wealth and prosperity that was oozing out of a land that was purportedly meant for farming.

The lesson is unmistakably clear. If we can persevere just a little longer, we will reap the fruit of our patience. Permit me to say this, if the two men who gave up had possessed the virtue of women, they would have been the ones to reap the benefits of having large treasures on their farm lands. Men need to cultivate the resilient and persevering nature of women.

WOMEN AND INTERCESSION

Women are good intercessors. In fact, they are the best intercessors. The way a woman is made makes her someone who can intercede. The intercessory ministry is fast becoming a forgotten ministry as most people are not prepared to function in the hidden ministry anymore.

An intercessor is someone who stands in gap for another. An intercessor is someone who goes through great pain in order to seek God's face during times of trial and affliction. An intercessor is someone who groans in prayer in order to see God's will being done in the lives of the objects of intercession. One of the qualities of an intercessor is the

59

ability to groan in prayer and travail. Such a kind of ministry is very tasking and laborious.

If there is any set of people that are best suited for the ministry of intercession, it is the womenfolk. Of all exercises on earth, none is as tedious, painful and energy sapping as the process of labour and child birth. The amount of energy which a woman uses to push out a baby is awesome. By the time a woman has gone through childbirth once, she is equipped to travail in prayer. Hence, women have found it naturally simple to spend long hours groaning in prayer in order to secure divine intervention for a particular issue or for a particular family.

> *For I have heard a voice as of a woman in travail , and the anguish as of her that bringeth forth her first child, the voice of the daughter of Zion, that bewaileth herself, that spreadeth her hands, saying, Woe is me now! for my soul is wearied because of murderers.* Jeremiah 4:31

> *We have heard the fame thereof: our hands wax feeble: anguish hath taken hold of us, and pain, as of a woman in travail.* Jeremiah 6:24
> *He shall see of the travail of his soul, and shall be satisfied: by his knowledge shall my righteous servant justify many; for he shall bear their iniquities.* Isaiah 53:11

> *A woman when she is in travail hath sorrow, because her hour is come: but as soon as*

60

she is delivered of the child, she rembereth no more the anguish, for joy that a man is born into the world. John 16:21

My little children, of whom I travail in birth again until Christ be formed in you,
Galatians 4:19

Intercession provides an opportunity for the woman to stand in the gap and make things happen.

And I sought for a man among them, that should make up the hedge, and stand in the gap before me for the land, that I should not destroy it: but I found none.
Ezekiel 22:30

Women have been called to stand in the gap for families, communities and churches. Every woman can convert her free moments to seasons of prayer. The best thing a woman can do is to make use of the sweet hour of prayer.

The song below means quite a lot to the interceding woman-
Sweet hour of prayer! sweet hour of prayer!
That calls me from a world of care,
And bids me at my Father's throne
Make all my wants and wishes known.
In seasons of distress and grief,
My soul has often found relief
And oft escaped the tempter's snare
By thy return, sweet hour of prayer!

Sweet hour of prayer! sweet hour of prayer!
The joys I feel, the bliss I share,
Of those whose anxious spirits burn
With strong desires for thy return!
With such I hasten to the place
Where God my Saviour shows His face,
And gladly take my station there,
And wait for thee, sweet hour of prayer!

Sweet hour of prayer! sweet hour of prayer!
Thy wings shall my petition bear
To Him whose truth and faithfulness
Engage the waiting soul to bless.
And since He bids me seek His face,
Believe His Word and trust His grace,
I'll cast on Him my every care,
And wait for thee, sweet hour of prayer!

Sweet hour of prayer! sweet hour of prayer!
May I thy consolation share,
Till, from Mount Pisgah's lofty height,
I view my home and take my flight:
This robe of flesh I'll drop and rise
To seize the everlasting prize;
And shout, while passing through the air,
"Farewell, farewell, sweet hour of prayer!"

Christian history has revealed that most of the ministries of prominent men of God have been kept in the realm of power, anointing and revival by prayer warriors who are mostly women. The way a woman travails in labour is the same way she succeeds in travailing in the place of prayer.

Prayer and intercession have been carried out predominantly in the Church by women. This is one area where God wants us to intercede for ministers of the gospel, churches, communities and nations. As we pray, the society will be preserved from corruption, churches will experience fresh waves of revival, individuals and churches will also experience divine peace and grace.

God is searching for female intercessors that will stop the tide of evil and usher great revival into homes, churches and nations. God wants to raise a new breed of women intercessors that will convert their latent energies to positive use for intercession and travailing in prayer. The more women get enlisted into the ministry of prayer, the more we will witness the power of God as of old. Such women will become a force to reckon with and God will be glorified.

PRAYER POINTS

1. Every satanic odour, chasing away my divine helper, disappear! in the name of Jesus.

2. Whatsoever is magnetizing the wrong people to my life, catch fire! in the name of Jesus.

3. Every connection between me and the spirit of anti-greatness, die! in the name of Jesus.

4. Garments of stagnation covering my greatness, catch fire! in the name of Jesus.

5. Every evil dream hindering my greatness, die! in the name of Jesus.

6. Every satanic power rewinding the clock of my greatness, fall down and die! in the name of Jesus.

7. Every satanic delay to my greatness, scatter! in the name of Jesus.

8. I receive power and divine connection to be great, in the name of Jesus.

9. I receive opportunity of a life time, in the name of Jesus.

10. I reject satanic breakthroughs assigned to divert my divine
    breakthroughs, in the name of Jesus.

11. Every door of opportunities the enemy has closed against my life in the time of ignorance, be opened by fire! in the name of Jesus.

12. All my helpers, receive power to help me, in the name of Jesus.

13. Let the door of worldwide breakthroughs be opened unto me, in the name of Jesus.

14. I receive breakthroughs of a lifetime, in the name of Jesus.

15. Every foundational rejection of my father's house, manifesting in my life now, die! in the name of Jesus.

16.   Every spirit of disfavour, lose your power upon my life, in the name of Jesus.

17.   Every demonic personality that has refused to let me go, die! in the name of Jesus.

NOTES:

Chapter

7

Women

Assets

To the

Church

*A woman when she is in travail hath
sorrow, because her hour is come; but
as soon as she is delivered of the child,
she remembereth no more the anguish,
for joy that a man is born into the world.*
John 16:21

Women are assets to the Church. The population of women will become an asset in every church. If we undertake the statistics of most churches, we will be surprised to discover that women are much more in number than men. The numerical strength of women can become a very wonderful asset. Most pastors are yet to learn what it takes to benefit from the female population of their congregation. Some pastors even complain that the women in their churches are too many. It is because such people do not know how to manage and make the best use of the energy of a growing female population.

From Bible days, women have been very active in the Church. Mary and Martha, Dorcas, Deborah, Pricilla, Elizabeth, Mary the mother of Jesus, Mary Magdalene, Prophetess Hannah, The four daughters of Philip, Lydia (a wealthy woman who gave Paul hospitality-Acts 16:13-15), Timothy's mother (Acts 16:1-2, 1 Timothy 1:5), Junia (Romans 15:7), Euodia and Syntyche (Philippians 4:2-3), Nympha (Colossians 4:15), Chloe (1 Corinthianss 1:11), Stephana (1 Corinthians 16:15), Phebe, (a deacon Romans- 16:1-2), and finally a rich lady whose name is not mentioned (2 John).

HIDDEN POTENTIALS
This long list shows that the early Church utilised the potentials of godly women, who played positive roles in the Church. As earlier stated, the role of women cannot be overemphasised. Women will remain an integral part of the Church.

The truth is that the contributions of women to the proclamation of the gospel of Jesus Christ are evident in the areas like: the prophetic ministry, the music ministry, evangelism, the ushering ministries, teaching, preaching, etc. If a woman like Deborah could be a judge in Israel and Lydia could be a prominent worker in the Church, no woman has any reason to fold her arms and say that the work of the ministry is for men alone.

My challenge to our women today is that we are not expected to sit idly at home or in the Church and watch while the men expend their energy in the work of the Lord. Rather, we are supposed to discover our place and purpose in God and walk into our glorious destiny.

As women, we can be part of an army of the Lord who makes a difference in the Church. As a woman, you can serve the Lord as one of the people who greet new comers. You can serve as an usher, a chorister, a deliverance minister, an administrative staff, a prophetess, a pastor, a women leader, an evangelist, a member of the literary department, a decorator, etc.

A NEW DAWN

It is time we took our rightful place. It is time we stepped into the shoes of Biblical heroines. Where are the intercessors? Where are the wailing women? Where are the scriptural prophetesses? Where are the women who will participate in carrying the ark of God? Where are the women who will throw all their weight into the work of their Father?

I am looking for Lady Evangelists. I am searching for women who are so sold out to the Lord that they would go out in search of area boys, area girls, street children and prostitutes.

Where are the members of the house fellowship who will get involved in the ministry of visitation? Where are the minister's wives who will build prayer engines for the ministries of their husbands? Where are the true daughters of destiny who will bring great changes into communities and nations?

Where are female ministers who will set the pace for integrity in ministry? Where are young ladies who will turn our campuses upside down for Christ? Where are the ladies with passion for school and youth ministry? Where are true women of God who will lead our men back to the Bible?

THE QUEST

These days, it is unfortunate that some minister's wives are the ones leading their husbands astray. My heart groans for the high spate of the loss of anointing among women. Can God not raise another Catherine Kullman? Can He not raise another Mother Crawford? Can God not give us another Catherine Booth? Where are the women with the prophetic anointing of Elijah? Where are modern day Deborah's? Where are the women who are ready to go through persecution?

Where are the women who are ready to pray until their wayward children come back home? Where are the women who would pray out their hearts until their unbelieving husbands get saved? Where are the women who will put on sack clothes and wail until backsliders are restored?

Where are the old-timers who will stand up for the

70

restoration of the old fashioned gospel? Where are our mothers in Israel who will bring up a new generation of godly youths? Where are the believers who are ready to support the cause of Christ? Where are the godly women who will back up the men who are working night and day to lift up the banner of Christ?

HELP, LORD!

One prayer that touches my heart can be found below;

> *Help, LORD; for the godly man ceaseth; for the faithful fail from among the children of men.* Psalm 12:1

The prayer point in my heart is;
"Help Lord, for the godly woman faileth. For real faithful women have become scarce."

Women are busy fighting each other. A lot of women have become incurable gossips. Christian women have become a divided community. Carnal, non-edifying and fleshly disagreements have taken precedence over godliness. Rather than go for deliverance, many women are busy finding faults with ministers. Women compete to outdo each other in fashion rather than cry out for the anointing of God. We are so busy trying to outdo others as far as latest fashions of the world rather than the inner beauty the Bible talks about. Our women have become too busy demonstrating carnality and ungodliness.

AN ALERT!

Our women are no longer praying for the beauty of Christ to be seen in their lives. Christian women no longer care about our true purpose in the Church. We are fast forgetting the fact that a good number of mainline Pentecostal denominations were birthed by praying, Holy Ghost anointed women. Pride, worldly fashion, competition, carnality and hypocrisy have taken over the hearts of our women. We no longer care about decency and modesty. A lot of women are now running after the things of the world, forgetting the Bible's exhortation in 1 Timothy 2:9-10;

> *In like manner also, that women adorn themselves in modest apparel, with shamefacedness and sobriety; not with broided hair, or gold, or pearls, or costly array; But (which becometh women professing godliness) with good works.*

REAL WOMEN

Where are the women of God? Where can we find modern day Dorcas'; who will sew dresses for the naked, provide food for the hungry and visit the sick in the hospitals? Where are the women who will sacrifice their comfort in order to meet the needs of others?

Where are the caring women? Where are the godly mothers? Where are the saintly sisters? Oh that God might restore to the Church, glorious women who will shake the community and move the Church forward. It is my prayer that God will visit our women and use them to usher fresh spirituality and revival into the Church.

Oh that God will help us to get to a place where the glory of God will be our passion; His will- our food and His work- our mission. Oh that God will help us to regain our lost tears in the place of prayer; renew our strength; and help us to get to a place where God himself will look at us and say; "These are my daughters, these are godly women." May God lead us to restoration, revival and renewal. May God give us women of wonder! AMEN!

PRAYER POINTS

1. Blood of Jesus, kill every evil mark on my body, in the name of Jesus.

2. Arrows of mistake and error, manifesting in my life in the presence of my helpers, die! in the name of Jesus.

3. Any evil done against my life, that is now making life difficult for me, die! in the name of Jesus.

4. Garments of disfavour covering my glory, catch fire! in the name of Jesus.

5. Satanic incantation working against my spirit man, perish by fire! in the name of Jesus.

6. Any power using my name against me, die! in the name of Jesus.

7. Any power in my father's house using my date of birth against my destiny, die, in the name of Jesus.

8. Anointing for favour from above, break the

yoke of disfavour in my life, in the name of Jesus.

9.   I walk out of the bondage of disfavour, in the name of Jesus.

10.   My heaven of favour, open now! in the name of Jesus.

11.   Every visible and invisible blockage on my way of progress, catch fire! in the name of Jesus.

12.   Every satanic immigration officer, manifesting in my dream, saying no to my fulfilment, die! in the name of Jesus.

13.   I receive power from above, to overcome every financial obstacle that is delaying my progress, in the name of Jesus.

14.   Every satanic document the enemy is using against me, catch fire! in the name of Jesus.

15.   You mistakes of the past, you will not destroy my testimony, in the name of Jesus.

NOTES:

_____
_____
_____
_____
_____
_____
_____
_____
_____
_____
_____
_____
_____
_____
_____
_____
_____
_____
_____
_____
_____
_____
_____

Chapter

8

Developing
Strong
Roots

*Husbands, love your wives, even as
Christ also loved the church, and gave
himself for it; Eph 5:25*

Women are endowed with the power of endurance. Research has shown that women can endure more than men. Endurance is a very strong virtue. God has made us with the ability to endure even when others would rather give up prematurely.

Thank God for women, many projects, family situations and circumstances would have ended up in failure. The fact that women are able to stick to whatever they are doing even in the face of obstacles and failures makes women outstanding. An average woman would rather endure than quit. "Quitters never win and winners never quit." When you refuse to quit, you are building up a strong testimony for yourself.

IMPORTANT LESSONS

I have learnt a lot of lessons in life. God passed me through several experiences which prepared me well enough to play my God appointed role. I knew the Lord at a tender age. When I was very young, it was clear in my spirit that God was calling me, but all I could do at that time was to get involved with music in the church. Quite early, I was singing in the choir and I was composing songs. Hence, I found myself in the church during my free moments.

Raised in a Pentecostal background, my late father of blessed memory brought us up with Spartan discipline. My friends knew that I was deeply religious. I had become so close to God that around age 12, the gifts of God started manifesting in my life. My passion for God did not allow me to go near what young people my age were doing around me. Then something happened that shocked me to my roots.

In spite of the fact that I experienced some setbacks when my high school results were seized and I began to ask God why, I had been very studious and was one of the good students in my class. With the shock of the seized results, I felt an urgent need for an encounter with the Saviour and that marked a turning point in my life.

I had a turning point with my Saviour, got saved and began to learn the principles of spiritual warfare. Going down memory lane, I can now see why God allowed initial setbacks to bring me to the foot of the cross. I was able to set my priorities right henceforth and by the time the Lord took centre stage in my life, I was able to pursue my academic career abroad.

The truth is that, it is important that every woman develops strong roots as nobody knows what lies ahead. You may see yourself as an ordinary woman today or just a local champion, but tomorrow, God can decide to catapult you to greatness and make you a woman of wonder. By the time God takes you up there, if you are not sufficiently prepared, you might not be able to cope.

A DRAMATIC CHANGE

Esther was an ordinary woman who never thought that she could become a queen. In divinely orchestrated circumstances, Queen Vashti misbehaved and a replacement was sought for her.

On the seventh day, when the heart of the king was merry with wine, he commanded Mehuman, Biztha, Harbona, Bigtha, and Abagtha, Zethar, and Carcas,

> *the seven chamberlains that served in the presence of Ahasuerus the king, To bring Vashti the queen before the king with the crown royal, to shew the people and the princes her beauty: for she was fair to look on. But the queen Vashti refused to come at the king's commandment by his chamberlains: therefore was the king very wroth, and his anger burned in him.*
> Esther 1:10-12

There was a problem in the palace which brought a dramatic change in the history of a great nation. One of the mysteries of the workings of the Almighty is that, He can create a problem in order to work out His agenda for your life. Initially, there was a great class distance between Queen Vashti and Esther, an ordinary orphan.

The word of Queen Vashti was law and no one thought that her place could become vacant. God can do anything to change history. Ordinarily, Vashti was not expected to misbehave, but, she had to put up a strange behaviour to give way for the divinely arranged queen in waiting. Meanwhile, Esther must have felt that her future was bleak, having lost her father and mother quite early in life.

> *And he brought up Hadassah, that is, Esther, his uncle's daughter: for she had neither father nor mother, and the maid was fair and beautiful; whom Mordecai, when her father and mother were dead, took for his own daughter.* Esther 2:7

A MYSTERY

Women often conclude that they cannot achieve anything just because they are handicapped or they lack certain opportunities. Strange enough, it was an uncle, Modeccai, who trained Esther. Here is another mystery- The ways of God are past finding out. How could a man have been used of God to train the future queen? The word of God is real;

> *O the depth of the riches both of the wisdom and knowledge of God! how unsearchable are his judgments, and his ways past finding out!* Romans 11:33

Esther was Modeccai's adopted daughter, yet, God had a glorious destiny for her. Thank God she complied with and accepted the training given to her. Another thing we should consider is the fact that following the natural scheme of things, Esther was not supposed to come anywhere near King Ahasuerus- a king of no mean status. His territory was huge as his kingdom covered Africa, Asia and the Middle-East.

> *Now it came to pass in the days of Ahasuerus, (this is Ahasuerus which reigned, from India even unto Ethiopia, over an hundred and seven and twenty provinces:)* Esther 1:1

DIVINE PREPARATION

Interestingly, there is a sort of paradox in the background of these two characters- Ahasuerus and Esther. Ahasuerus was too noble and too rich to come near a slave. Esther was a captive during the reign of Nebuchadnezzar the king of Babylon.

> *Who had been carried away from Jerusalem with the captivity which had been carried away with Jeconiah king of Judah, whom Nebuchadnezzar the king of Babylon had carried away.* Esther 2:6

However, God was preparing her for greatness. Consider this fact- When God is preparing you for a great position in life, you might have to undergo rigorous discipline, but if you can follow the divine pathway, you will wake up one day and discover that you have become a celebrity overnight. As Vashti misbehaved, the king sacked her in order to avoid a bad precedence being set.

> *Then the king said to the wise men, which knew the times, (for so was the king's manner toward all that knew law and judgment: And the next unto him was Carshena, Shethar, Admatha, Tarshish, Meres, Marsena, and Memucan, the seven princes of Persia and Media, which saw the king's face, and which sat the first in the kingdom;) What shall we do unto the queen Vashti according to law, because she hath not performed the commandment of the king Ahasuerus by the chamberlains? And Memucan answered before the king and the princes, Vashti the queen hath not done wrong to the king only, but also to all the princes,*

and to all the people that are in all the provinces of the king Ahasuerus. For this deed of the queen shall come abroad unto all women, so that they shall despise their husbands in their eyes, when it shall be reported, The king Ahasuerus commanded Vashti the queen to be brought in before him, but she came not. Likewise shall the ladies of Persia and Media say this day unto all the king's princes, which have heard of the deed of the queen. Thus shall there arise too much contempt and wrath. If it please the king, let there go a royal commandment from him, and let it be written among the laws of the Persians and the Medes, that it be not altered, That Vashti come no more before king Ahasuerus; and let the king give her royal estate unto another that is better than she. Esther 1:13 19

What would have become of Esther if she had lived carelessly when she was growing up? This would have stood against her when she was vying for the post of a first lady. Parental discipline and certain experiences generally prepare us for the future. This should be considered by today's younger women.

MY BACKGROUND

My background offered me only one option when I was growing up- serious discipline. My father was a strict disciplinarian who believed that all his children should embrace hard work. The Church environment also presented another type of discipline which made it impossible for me to engage in worldly activities. I was either studying or serving the Lord in the Church. Like Esther, I did not know what God had in store for me.

My consecration to the Lord was so evident to my neighbours and classmates that they gave me a nickname, 'Omo C.A.C.' (The CAC girl) meaning that I was never expected to misbehave. It was not so easy to be different from others, but I chose the path of righteousness. I also knew that the hand of God was upon my life; hence, I was very careful. Either when I was studying in Nigeria or outside Nigeria, I did not compromise my faith.

By the time I got married to my husband, the General Overseer, M.F.M.M. the call of God became stronger. In those days, I was not even a minister of the gospel. We started the fellowship in a small way. My husband at that time was working as a medical research scientist and it did not really dawn on me that one day, I will pursue a global ministry alongside him.

ALONE WITH GOD
I spent most of my free moments alone with God. I could not just pick up any friend. Yes I was lonely, but I knew that God was preparing me for something great. I could not behave the way I wanted. I could not mix with others who were flamboyant. I knew that I was a daughter of destiny. I knew that God was keeping me for a time in the future when there would be an explosion. All I knew was that I took interest in people's spiritual welfare.

I would close the door and spend time praying and interceding for people. Early in my marriage, I also learnt how to pray for my husband. Since he was busy ministering most of the time, I developed a secret intercessory ministry for him. While I was praying for him, I was also asking God to prepare me for the future. Unknown to me, God was busy working on me because He has a great agenda and task for me.

LED BY GOD

While I was growing up, God taught me the importance of Christian virtues. People often wonder how I met my husband. While I was quite young, my husband was the choir director of our church then, I was just one of the young members. All of a sudden, we no longer saw 'Brother Daniel' as we called him then. Nonetheless, I continued to serve the Lord together with others. Personally, I had even forgotten about Brother Daniel. All we knew was that he had gone abroad for further studies. By the time he came back, a few of us who saw him as our role model came around him again. One thing led to another and I became the young girl who would marry our former choir director.

I thought that was all there was to it. My husband started a small school of prayer; a kind of prayer meeting to teach people the basics of prayer, the importance of spiritual warfare, as well as give people opportunity to pray and secure divine intervention for their needs. Then, he also led us into deliverance. We thought we were just called to do something little for the Lord, but by the time we moved from Old Yaba Road to the present international headquarters site, there was a great explosion. That was the point when I started praying like never before.

THE NEED FOR HUMILITY

There was a sort of fear in my heart when it dawned on me that a lot of members would look up to me as their spiritual mother. That made me to see a greater need for humility. Therefore, I spent time asking the Lord to help me.

If you ask me, I would have preferred to lead a quiet life, but in spite of my preferences, God has chosen to bring me into the limelight. Now I have to minister to people in the areas of prayer, counselling, deliverance, etc. I thank God that God prepared me adequately and made everything around my background to cooperate with His plans for my destiny.

The lesson we can all learn here is that today, you may be a quiet and an unassuming Esther hiding somewhere, but if you allow God to work on you, soon, He will put you on a throne where you will become a divine answer to the need of millions of people all over the world. Don't ever complain that God is too harsh on you or that your parents are too strict. The more glorious your future is, the more time God will spend on you. At the moment, God is nurturing and developing a future Queen Esther somewhere, just allow God to have His way in your life. By the time God is finished with you, every experience will count, all training will matter, and everything God did to make you a woman of wonder will be justified.

As God is searching for women whom He would use in this generation, may He find you ready, prepared and willing. Amen!

PRAYER POINTS

1. I use the fire of God and the blood of Jesus to surround my destiny, in the name of Jesus.

2. Every power, working against the fulfilment of my destiny, be disgraced! in the name of Jesus.

3. I command my destiny to reject every bewitchment, in the name of Jesus.

4. I deliver my destiny from the grip of destiny killers, in the name of Jesus.

5. Every evil done to my destiny by household wickedness, be reversed now! in the name of Jesus.

6. Every vessel of destiny killers, fashioned against my destiny, fall down and die! in the name of Jesus.

7. Let the ground open now and swallow all destiny killers working against me, in the name of Jesus.

8. Every evil gathering against my destiny, be scattered! in the name of Jesus.

9. My destiny, you will not manage poverty, in the name of Jesus.

10. My destiny, you will not manage failure, in the name of Jesus.

11. I command my destiny to begin to change to the best now, in the name of Jesus.

12. My head will not carry evil load, in the name of Jesus.

13. Every enemy of progress in my life, fall down and die now! in the name of Jesus.

14. I reject every evil manipulation against my destiny, in the name of Jesus.

15. I paralyse every activity of destiny killers, in every area of my life, in the name of Jesus.

16. I smash every giant of 'almost there' to pieces, in the name of Jesus.

17. I destroy every castle of backwardness, in the name of Jesus.

18. I receive the anointing to destroy every destiny killer, in the name of Jesus.

NOTES:

Chapter

9

Women

and a

Happy
Marriage

*Husbands, love your wives, and be not
bitter against them. Col 3:19*

Marriage is teamwork. The Bible has assigned different roles to each couple. The husband has roles and the wife also has roles. The children too are not left out. There is no denying the fact that the husband is the head of the home, but the role of a woman is also important.

> *Wives, submit yourselves unto your own husbands, as unto the Lord. For the husband is the head of the wife, even as Christ is the head of the church: and he is the saviour of the body. Therefore as the church is subject unto Christ, so let the wives be to their own husbands in every thing. Husbands, love your wives, even as Christ also loved the church, and gave himself for it; That he might sanctify and cleanse it with the washing of water by the word, That he might present it to himself a glorious church, not having spot, or wrinkle, or any such thing; but that it should be holy and without blemish. So ought men to love their wives as their own bodies. He that loveth his wife loveth himself.* Ephesians 5:22-28

Marriage has secrets. There are certain things men and women can do to make the home happy, blessed, stable and prosperous. If each member of the family would play their individual roles well, marriage would be glorious. However, the problem is that husbands blame their wives while wives blame their husbands. Shifting blames would not take us anywhere, but when each member of the family settles down to carry out their own functions, the home will become a wonderful place to live in.

Of all the roles, the role of the wife is quite significant. While the husband is instructed to love the wife, the wife is mandated to be submissive. When roles are carried out meticulously especially by the women, the divorce rate will be minimal. It takes two to have a quarrel. It takes more than one party to bring up a problem in the home. In an era when the divorce rate is very high, we need to redefine the role of women in a successful marriage.

Way back in the fifties, the divorce rate in the Church was lower than the divorce rate in the world. In this generation however, the divorce rate in the Church is the same as the divorce rate in the world. Women though quite unassuming and humble, form the bedrock of the family. No matter what is going on in the family, a woman can act as a stabilising force.

The following are secrets of marital happiness:

1. **The women must be submissive-** There is nothing that puts men off like lack of submission. Marriage is partnership; both the husband and the wife come together as partners in a mutual agreement. Marriage should not be a forum for competition, rivalry or struggle for leadership. According to God's pattern, the husband is the head while the wife is expected to follow the leadership of the head. The Bible teaches that women should have one quality- **submission!**

One of the causes of conflict in the home can be traced to attempts by women to struggle for superiority. When you respect your husband as a woman, you will submit to him in all areas of life. The scriptural order is that the husband leads under God, while the wife follows with humility and godly reverence. When there is submission, things would go on normally. The wife will cooperate fully with her husband by following the instructions and the directions given by him.

A submissive wife will naturally enjoy the attention and affection of her husband. You must nurture the home by demonstrating uncommon humility and submission. God will definitely defend your interest as a woman when you submit to your husband as the Church submits to Christ.

2. **The wife should take note of the fact that her spouse belongs to God-** Hence, she should be ready to give an account of the relationship to God. The husband and the wife are supposed to relate together scripturally. When the wife submits, the husband will naturally show love, affection and care.

3. **The wife must treat her husband in the way she would like to be treated-** Kindness begets kindness, respect begets respect. Everyone will reap the fruits they sow. What couples sow is what they will reap. You must give to your husband what you want him to give back to you. If your spouse were to pay you back in your coin, what kind of treatment will you deserve? As a woman, you must desire and decide to know your partner better. This will help you to understand him better and you will be

able to treat him the way he would love to be treated. Just as you expect your husband to study you and begin to do what pleases you, you must study him and begin to do what pleases him. Your ability to please your husband will draw corresponding response from him. Do not use bad language on your husband. Picture in your husband the ideal character. Let your conversation, conduct and attitude show that you are committed to doing the best to make your husband happy. Every woman should therefore be a student in the school of managing the husband effectively. By the time you succeed in doing things that gladdens your husband's heart, he will begin to put up positive changes. I am yet to see a wife who sowed good seeds in the life of her husband and ends up reaping bad fruits.

* One of the secrets of success in marriage is to look away from what you expect your husband to do to make you happy and begin to make serious efforts towards making him happy.

The Bible says;
Cast thy bread upon the waters: for thou shalt find it after many days. Ecclesiates 11:1

No seed sown is wasted; no effort is useless; and no labour is lost. What you do today will yield wonderful fruits tomorrow. Just keep sowing. One of these days, God will reward you and your contribution as a woman will surely pay off.

4.   **Women should ensure that the altar of prayer is aglow with fire-** Although devotions and prayers are supposed to be led by the husband, yet the woman can complement the husband's role and leadership. She can take charge when he is away or slightly indisposed. A survey has shown that couples who pray together will experience divorce threats that are incredibly low, in fact, less than one percent. Praying together is therefore the key. Praying together is a sign of unity. It is also proof that the couple stands together united before the throne of grace.

Prayer grants the couple the opportunity to appreciate God's goodness, seek His forgiveness, ask for His mercy and draw upon His grace. Prayer creates an incredible bond between couples. Prayer heals deep wounds. Prayer affords couples the opportunity to appreciate the Almighty. Prayer gives husbands and wives the chance to hold hands and agree on what they want from God.

Prayer will open closed doors and allow couples to move in and possess their possessions. With prayer, doors of failure will be closed, and the strength of the Almighty will be tapped. By praying together, the Lord will bless your efforts. The Lord will bless each couple as they unite in prayer.

Through prayer, the wife will discover that all things are possible. Prayer will keep away satanic agents. Therefore, every wise woman will ensure that prayer is number one activity in the family. Prayer will make all things possible and the God who brought you together as a couple will make all things beautiful in His time.

Happy is that woman who creates time to pray alone and encourages family prayer, since she knows that prayer is the master key that opens the door of marital success.

PRAYER POINTS

1. Every anti progress spirit, be bound by chain of fire! in the name of Jesus.

2. Every satanic prison warden, fall down and die! in the name of Jesus.

3. I shall not crash in the race of life, in the name of Jesus.

4. My progress shall not be terminated, in the name of Jesus.

5. Let my life be too hot for the enemy to handle, in the name of Jesus.

6. Every power, set up to pull me down spiritually, be disgraced! in the name of Jesus.

7. Every power, set up to pull me down physically, be disgraced! in the name of Jesus.

8. Every power, set up to pull down my marriage, be disgrace!, in the name of Jesus.

9. Every power set up to pull my finances down, be disgraced, in the name of Jesus.

10. No 'progress arrester' shall prevail over my life, in the name of Jesus.

11. I receive power to excel in every area of my life, in the name of Jesus.

12. I shall mount up with wings as the eagles, in the name of Jesus.

13. I withdraw my wealth from the hand of the bondwoman and her children, in the name of Jesus.

14. I will not squander my divine opportunities, in the name of Jesus.

15. I must pray to get results in this programme, in Jesus' name.

16. I dismantle any power working against my efficiency, in the name of Jesus.

17. I refuse to lock the door of blessings against myself, in the name of Jesus.

18. I refuse to be a wandering star, in the name of Jesus.

19. I refuse to appear to disappear, in the name of Jesus.

NOTES:

Chapter

10

The

Glorious
Woman

*The heart of her husband doth safely
trust in her, so that he shall have no need
of spoil.
She will do him good and not evil all
the days of her life, Prov. 31:11-12*

ncluded in this book is a practical guide to what it takes to become a glorious woman by drawing upon the principles that are embedded in Proverbs 31. The truth is that, every woman has the characteristics of the Proverbs 31 woman inherent in her. These characteristics must be released and brought to the fore. Let us go to the school of the glorious woman.

Course One
BUILDING VALUES
* **PRACTICAL TRAITS:**
    * She is a glorious woman.
    * She is priceless.
    * She is a crown to her husband.
    * She belongs to a rare breed.
    * She is virtuous.
    * She is a woman of substance.

* **THE SCRIPTURAL FOUNDATION**
    Who can find a virtuous woman? for her price is far above rubies. Pro 31:10

* **THE SCHOOL OF GLORIOUS WOMEN**
There is a search for glorious women. The world is waiting for truly virtuous women. The woman with excellent attributes would always   stand out.   She would be so loaded with inner qualities that she would be priceless.

* **STEPS TO TAKE:**
1.   You must evaluate your character.
2.   You must pay attention to your inner values.
3.   You must develop godly virtues.
4.   You must maintain you quality of character.
* **PRAYER POINTS:**

99

1. O Lord, visit me and transform my character.
2. My Father, make me the virtuous woman whom the world is looking for.
3. *(For Bachelors)* O Lord, give me a virtuous woman.
4. *(For Husbands)* O Lord, take my wife to your spiritual laboratory and transform her.
5. I refuse to be a problem to my husband and my generation.

Course Two
BUILDING TRUST

*   **PRACTICAL TRAITS**
    *   She is trustworthy.
    *   She is of noble character.
    *   She is an asset to her husband.

*   **THE SCRIPTURAL FOUNDATION**
    The heart of her husband doth safely trust in her, so that he shall have no need of spoil. She will do him good and not evil all the days of her life. Prov 31:11-12

*   **THE SCHOOL OF GLORIOUS WOMEN**

A glorious woman is a woman of sterling qualities. The world needs such women today. Men are crying for women who would be assets not liabilities. When you are an asset to your husband, that man will be happy for life. This explains why it is said that, "Behind every successful man is a woman." Because you are a glorious woman, your husband should trust in you, should prosper at whatever business he does, and should experience goodness all his days.

* STEPS TO TAKE:
1. You must build trust.
2. You must avoid shady characteristics.
3. You must make sure that you contribute positively to your husband and community.
4. Your overall attitude must instil confidence in your husband.

* PRAYER POINTS:
1. My Father, make me a glorious woman, in the name of Jesus.
2. O Lord, help me to build a trustworthy character, in the name of Jesus.
3. My Father, make me an asset to my husband and community.
4. I will do my husband good and not evil, in the name of Jesus.
5. O Lord, make me, mould me and build me into a glorious woman, in the name of Jesus.

Course Three
BUILDING SKILLS

*   PRACTICAL TRAITS
*   She is industrious.
*   She has good domestic skills.
*   She works.
*   She does not give in to idleness.
*   She is willing to get her hands dirty with manual work.

* THE SCRIPTURAL FOUNDATION
She seeketh wool, and flax, and worketh willingly with her hands. Pro 31:13

101

* **THE SCHOOL OF GLORIOUS WOMEN**

We often say a lot about the prayer life, the devotion and the spirituality of a godly woman, but here, God has given us a portrait of the practical attributes of a godly woman. There are practical things a woman must do to be called a glorious woman. Such a woman must be hard working and skilful. The woman described above shows unusual dexterity in artisan. Such a woman would be able to make things like hat, be able to knit, bake and do other things that will keep her hands busy.

* **STEPS TO TAKE:**
1. You must learn new skills like soap making, batik, hat making, etc.
2. You can enrol in a fashion and design school.
3. You can learn how to make simples soaps and detergents.
4. You can enrol in a nearby catering school.
5. You must convert your free time to a time when you can put your hands to practical uses.

* **PRAYER POINTS:**
1. O Lord, anoint my hands. in Jesus' name.
2. My Father, open my eyes to practical things I can do with my hands, in Jesus' name.
3. O Lord, let these fingers of mine bring blessings to my home, in Jesus' name.
4. I refuse to eat the bread of idleness, in the name of Jesus.

Course Four
BUILDING AN INTERNATIONAL BUSINESS
* **PRACTICAL TRAITS:**
    * She is not limited to her local environment.
    * She can explore the possibilities of an international business.
    * She knows how to go very far to purchase food for the family.
    * She is very skillful in knowing where to get what her family needs from far and near.

* **THE SCRIPTURAL FOUNDATION**
  She is like the merchants' ships; she bringeth her food from afar. Pro 31:14

* **THE SCHOOL OF GLORIOUS WOMEN**
A glorious woman is a woman who combines spirituality with beneficial activities. She is as busy as the merchant's ship. Whatever will be of benefit to her family is explored by her. Additionally, she is able to bring her food from afar. She knows what it takes to meet the nutritional needs of her family.
* **STEPS TO TAKE:**
1. She must be ready to read books on profitable businesses.
2. If possible, she can consider international business.
3. She must be able to source food items from both nearby and distant markets.

* **PRAYER POINTS:**
1. O Lord, give me positive connections that will advance my home, in the name of Jesus.

2. My Father, give me the strength to go far in seeking the best for my home, in Jesus' name.

3. I receive wisdom to discover, source and provide good food for my family, in the name of Jesus.

4. Anointing for international business, fall upon me! in the name of Jesus.

5. My family will not remain at the valley, in the name of Jesus.

Course Five
BUILDING INDUSTRY
* **PRACTICAL TRAITS**
    * She is an early riser.
    * She is not lacking in the area of giving good food to the entire family.
    * She controls her children and her servants.
    * She is not lazy.
    * She does not abandon household chores to servants and children.

* **THE SCRIPTURAL FOUNDATION**
    She riseth also while it is yet night, and giveth meat to her household, and a portion to her maidens. Pro 31:15

* **THE SCHOOL OF GLORIOUS WOMEN**
God is interested in the domestic life of a glorious woman. The spirituality of such a woman is also measured by how she is able to get up early in order to strike a balance between the various activities of the day. The glorious woman must not hide under spirituality and excuse her laziness.

* STEPS TO TAKE:
1. You must become an early riser.
2. Never joke with your family's meals.
3. Do not abandon your kitchen to your servants.
4. You must provide food for your family and your servants.
5. As a glorious woman, God can so bless you that your domestic duties will increase and consequently you will need to pray for funds to hire domestic servants.

* PRAYER POINTS:
1. O Lord, bless me indeed after the order of Jabez, in Jesus' name.
2. O Lord, enlarge my coast in the name of Jesus.
3. I refuse to allow laziness to hinder my progress, in the name of Jesus.
4. O Lord, give me wisdom to take charge of my domestic duties, in Jesus' name.

Course Six
BUIDLING BUSINESS ACUMEN
* PRACTICAL TRAITS:
- * She is intelligent.
- * She develops a good business sense.
- * She explores extra earnings for the family.
- * She considers profitable investments.
- * She is an astute business lady.

* THE SCRIPTURAL FOUNDATION
She considereth a field, and buyeth it: with the fruit of her hands she planteth a vineyard. Proverbs 31:16

* **THE SCHOOL OF GLORIOUS WOMEN**

The world has assigned all the good qualities to men, believing that women are supposed to stay at home and do nothing, but the glorious woman is here to prove this as wrong. You must develop and manifest intelligence that would evaluate a piece of property and buy it. It takes a wise woman to use her own earnings to buy a field and plant a vineyard for the benefit of her family. No matter how rich your husband is, you can contribute to the wealth of your home.

* **STEPS TO TAKE:**
1. You can undertake a research into businesses you can do to augment the income of the family.
2. You can by items and properties with wisdom.
3. You don't need to depend on borrowing.
4. You can develop new streams of income to make life comfortable.

* **PRAYER POINTS:**
1. O Lord, lead me into financial independence, in Jesus' name.
2. I receive the anointing for business success, in the name of Jesus.
3. O Lord, show me what to do in order to lead my family in to prosperity, in Jesus' name.
4. O Lord, change my situation, in the name of Jesus.
5. I decree a change in my family, in the name of Jesus.

Course Seven
BUILDING STRENGTH

* **PRACTICAL TRAITS:**
  * She is energetic.
  * She does not give in to weakness and laziness.
  * She embraces hard work.
  * She is able to cope with ever increasing domestic duties.
  * Laziness or tiredness are not able to weaken her bones.

* **THE SCRIPTURAL FOUNDATION**
  She girdeth her loins with strength, and strengtheneth her arms. Proverbs 31:17

* **THE SCHOOL OF GLORIOUS WOMEN**

The glorious woman is able to explore her strength to make her home conducive. She is strong and always in good health. She knows the type of food and food supplements to take to keep a healthy lifestyle. She is not afraid of physical work. She undertakes her duties rigorously and her arms are strong for her tasks. True to the nature of a glorious woman, she is strong and tiredness is never allowed to rob her of achievements.

* **STEPS TO TAKE:**
1. You must be an energetic woman.
2. You must be a woman who works very hard.
3. There must be strength in your carriage.
4. You must convert your hidden energy to productive uses.

107

* **PRAYER POINTS:**
1. O Lord, strengthen me in every area of my life, in Jesus' name.
2. My inner man, receive fire! in Jesus' name.
3. O Lord, send your fire to my bones and energise me.
4. I refuse to receive the arrow of laziness.
5. O Lord, guard me with strength.
6. Holy Ghost fire, strengthen my arms, in the name of Jesus.

Course Eight
BUILDING HOME-MADE BUSINESSES

* **PRACTICAL TRAITS:**
    * She excels in business.
    * She carries out profitable trading.
    * She is able to work extra hours during seasons of high demand.
    * She demonstrates special skills.
    * She is a model of industry.

* **THE SCRIPTURAL FOUNDATION**
  She perceiveth that her merchandise is good: her candle goeth not out by night. She layeth her hands to the spindle, and her hands hold the distaff. Proverbs 31:18-19

* **THE SCHOOL OF GLORIOUS WOMEN**
The school of glorious women is made up of women who are ready to give the world a new picture of what it takes to be a woman of virtue. Rather than gossip and sit idly at home, a glorious woman is so busy that she has to work

extra hours. Her product is so good that demand forces her to burn the midnight oil. Her hands are busy and her fingers are occupied with activities that enhance the value of her family. The kind of business she does, does not take her away from her home. She is able to do what makes for the well-being of her family.

* **STEPS TO TAKE:**
1. You must be involved in profitable business.
2. You must find out what you can do to keep yourself busy.
3. You must get involved in things that will isolate depression, laziness and idleness.
4. You must excel in the business you are involved in.

* **PRAYER POINTS:**
1. Anointing of excellence, fall upon me in the name of Jesus.
2. O Lord, make me profitable in my business.
3. O Lord, advertise my products and bless me, in the name of Jesus.
4. You my hands, you shall not be attacked by evil powers.

Course Nine
BUILDING KINDNESS AND CHARITY
* **PRACTICAL TRAITS:**
   * She is a giver.
   * She shares with the poor and needy.
   * She is a good example in the area of charity.
   * She knows what is meant by; "It is more blessed to give than to receive."

* **THE SCRIPTURAL FOUNDATION**
  She stretcheth out her hand to the poor;
  yea, she reacheth forth her hands to the
  needy. Pro 31:20

* **THE SCHOOL OF GLORIOUS WOMEN**

You can be called a student in the school of glorious women when what you do earns a profitable income and you are willing to share these blessings with the poor and the needy. Some women are busy acquiring wealth but they neglect the poor and needy around them. This is not good. A glorious woman should be a giver. She should be known for her generosity. If you want God to bless you, you must find practical ways of reaching out to the needy.

* **STEPS TO TAKE:**
1. You must give to the needy.
2. You must be a blessing to the poor.
3. Something must pass through your hands to your needy neighbours.
4. You must be an outgoing woman.
5. You must cast off the garment of selfishness by reaching forth your hands to the needy.
6. Take a look at your wardrobe and bring out certain things for the poor and needy neighbours.
7. Go to your kitchen and store and bring out something with which you can feed the poor.
8. Take a look at your account or safe and bring out something to share with the poor.

* **PRAYER POINTS:**
1. O Lord, give me the heart of a giver.

110

2.   My Father, help me to reach out to the needy.
3.   O Lord, make me a channel of blessing today.
4.   My Father, let my life be an encouragement to the poor and needy.

Course Ten
BUILDING CORE DOMESTIC VALUES
*   PRACTICAL TRAITS:
*   She takes meticulous look at the dress patterns of the entire family.
*   She is a woman who sets her priority. She refuses to be sidetracked from her domestic responsibilities.
*   She is busy at home. (Titus 2:5)
*   She makes adequate provisions for her home.

*   **THE SCRIPTURAL FOUNDATION**
She is not afraid of the snow for her household: for all her household are clothed with scarlet. Proverbs 31:21

*   **THE SCHOOL OF GLORIOUS WOMEN**
A glorious woman is full of wisdom. She is so intelligently endowed that she does not neglect any aspect of her family life. Her household is clothed with scarlet. The word scarlet refers to warm clothing. She is aware of different seasons; therefore she is not afraid of changing weather conditions as she has provided adequate clothing for her family.

*   **STEPS TO TAKE:**
1.   You need to read books on uses of various fabrics.

111

2. You must study various weather conditions.
3. You need to make preparations for every season.
4. You must be so sufficiently prepared that seasonal diseases, harsh weather conditions, and various seasons of life do not constitute a threat to your family.

* **PRAYER POINTS:**
1. O Lord, make me the pillar of my home in the name of Jesus.
2. O Lord, deliver me from negligence and carelessness, in the name of Jesus.
3. Wisdom from above, fall upon me! in the name of Jesus.
4. Skill from the throne of grace, my life is available, fall upon me! in the name of Jesus.
5. My Father, help me to prepare my home against all eventualities.

Course Eleven
BUILDING EXCELLENCE
* **PRACTICAL TRAITS:**
* She is a symbol of royalty.
* She believes that only the best is good enough for her.
* She is a stickler for finesse.
* She puts on the best types of dresses.
* She has an eye for designer items.
* She is not so busy to the point that her appearance is repulsive.
* She has time for herself.
* She has time for her home.

* She has a knack for excellent decorations.

* **THE SCRIPTURAL FOUNDATION**
 She maketh herself coverings of tapestry; her clothing is silk and purple.
 Proverbs 31:22

* **THE SCHOOL OF GLORIOUS WOMEN**
Members of the school of glorious woman are women who have maximised their potentials and cultivated the habits of succeeding. They are able to get to a class where their physical appearance matters. Hence, they have to go for the best of everything. When you become a member of the class of those who have achieved excellence, your dressing will change. Somebody has said, "Dress the way you want to be addressed." Let your outward appearance be characterised by excellence and royalty.

* **STEPS TO TAKE:**
1. Re-evaluate your wardrobe.
2. Introduce finesse and excellence into your furniture and beddings.
3. Give your husband a surprise by giving him excellent modelling of your home.
4. Shop for clothings that are characterised by quality.
5. Dress as if you are the richest woman in your community.
6. Avoid extremes, be moderate.

* **PRAYER POINTS:**
1. My Father, give me ideas that will transform my life, in the name of Jesus.

2. O Lord, change my status and move me forward by fire, in the name of Jesus.
3. O Lord, send down prosperity and make me a specimen of your glory, in the name of Jesus.

Course Twelve
BUILDING SHARED RESPONSIBILITIES
PRACTICAL TRAITS:
* She complements her husband's efforts.
* While she pursues excellence at home, her husband is a symbol of excellence at the gates.
* She makes her husband proud.
* She plays her role well.
* Her inputs in her husband's life earn him respect in his work place.

THE SCRIPTURAL FOUNDATION
Her husband is known in the gates, when he sitteth among the elders of the land.
Proverbs. 31:23

THE SCHOOL OF GLORIOUS WOMEN
One of the attributes of the glorious woman is the ability to contribute meaningfully to her husband's success. The goal of the glorious woman is to add value to the life of her husband. She is supposed to be so productive and positive that her husband will automatically earn respect among the elders of the land, and even in his work place.

STEPS TO TAKE:
1. Make efforts towards giving your husband a Good public image.

114

2. Give your husband peace of mind as he pursues his career.
3. Let your husband be proud of you.
4. Be a pillar behind your husband.

· **PRAYER POINTS:**
1. Father Lord, make me a pillar behind my husband, in the name of Jesus.
2. O God, let my life build for my husband, a good public image, in the name of Jesus.
3. I shall not bring shame to my husband, in the name of Jesus.
4. By fire by force, my life shall be a lift to my husband, in Jesus' name.

Course Thirteen
BUILDING HONOUR AND RESPECT
* **PRACTICAL TRAITS:**
   * She is a woman of dignity.
   * · She makes adequate preparation.
   * She is a good planner.
   * She has foresight.
   * She is not overtaken by events.

THE SCRIPTURAL FOUNDATION
Strength and honour are her clothing;
and she shall rejoice in time to come.
Proverbs 31:25

· **THE SCHOOL OF GLORIOUS WOMEN**
The glorious woman is respected by all. She is not frivolous or embarrassing in her conduct. She is woman of strength. She is also a woman of honour. Her life is

115

characterised by wisdom and foresight. She is not lousy in any way.

- **STEPS TO TAKE**
1. Make deliberate efforts to build honour.
2. Retain your dignity.
3. Avoid things that can tarnish your image.
4. Remember you are a glorious woman.
5. Let your comportment and carriage portray you as a woman of wonder.

PRAYER POINTS:
1. Father Lord, give me strength and health, in the name of Jesus.
2. O God of glory, envelope with honour and respect.
3. My Father, continue to fill me with wisdom that will make me excel in life, in Jesus' name.
4. O Lord, I am depending on you, help me.
5. I shall not fail, in the name of Jesus.

Course Fourteen
BUILDING WISDOM

* **PRACTICAL TRAITS:**
    * She is and embodiment of wisdom.
    * She speaks with wisdom.
    * Her words are characterised by courtesy and kindness.

- **THE SCRIPTURAL FOUNDATION**
She openeth her mouth with wisdom;
and in her tongue is the law of kindness.
Proverbs 31:26

THE SCHOOL OF GLORIOUS WOMEN

The school of glorious women has vacancies for women who are loaded with wisdom. In the Church today, we need ladies and mothers who will display wisdom in everything they do. We sincerely need women whose conversations are characterised by courtesy and kindness, women whose words edify and whose words are seasoned with grace. May God give us women who are filled with wisdom. Amen!

STEPS TO TAKE:
1.   Pray for divine wisdom.
2.   Decide that you will only open your mouth to speak wise words.
3.   Let kindness rule your conversation.
4.   Avoid any form of foolishness or harshness in your conducts and speech.

PRAYER POINTS:
1.   O Lord, touch my lips, in Jesus' name.
2.   Anointing for wisdom, fall upon my life! in the name of Jesus.
3.   O thou law of kindness, transform my tongue! in the name of Jesus.
4.   I refuse to speak foolish words, in the name of Jesus.
5.   My mouth shall not glorify the devil, in the name of Jesus.

Course Fifteen
BUILDING APPRECIATION
* **PRACTICAL TRAITS:**
    * She is a woman who has practically earned appreciation.

117

* She has a good impact on her children.
* She has a good impact on her husband.
* She puts up lots of actions for which she can be praised.
* Her own works praise her.
* She reaps the fruits of her labour.

· THE SCRIPTURAL FOUNDATION
She looketh well to the ways of her household, and eateth not the bread of idleness. Her children arise up, and call her blessed; her husband also, and he praiseth her. Many daughters have done virtuously, but thou excellest them all. Proverbs 31:27-29

THE SCHOOL OF GLORIOUS WOMEN
The school of glorious women requires women who are so faithful in discharging their duties that they earn the admiration of their family. Such women are praised by their children and their husbands. They can be described as women of excellence. They shall surely reap the fruits of their labour.

· STEPS TO TAKE:
1. Focus your attention on things to do to earn the appreciation of your children.
2. Focus your energy on what to do to make your husband proud of you.
3. Make 'excellence' your watch word.
4. Earn commendation not condemnation.

PRAYER POINTS
1. Father Lord, give me the wisdom to bring up my Children successfully.

2.   O Lord, teach me what to do to earn the appreciation of my husband, in the name of Jesus.

3.   My father and my God, make me to excel, in the name of Jesus.

4.   I reject failure and shame, in the name of Jesus.

5.   Let ministering angels bring customers and favour to me, in the name of Jesus.

6.   Anyone occupying my seat of prosperity, clear away! in the name of Jesus.

7.   Lord, make a way for me in the land of the living.

8.   I bind the spirit of fake and useless investment, in the name of Jesus.

9.   All unsold materials, be sold with profit, in the name of Jesus.

10.   Let all business failures be converted to success, in the name of Jesus.

11.   Every curse on my hands and legs, be broken! In the name of Jesus.

12.   O Lord, embarrass me with abundance in every area of my life.

13.   Every effect of strange money, affecting my prosperity, be neutralized! in the name of Jesus.

14.   Let brassy heavens break forth and bring rain, in Jesus' name.

15.   I break the control of every spirit of poverty over my life, in the name of Jesus.

16.   Lord Jesus, anoint my eyes to see the hidden riches of this world.

17.   Lord Jesus, advertise your breakthroughs in my life.

18.   Let the riches of the ungodly be transferred unto my hands, in the name of Jesus.

19.   I will rise above the unbelievers around me, in the name of Jesus.

20.   O Lord, make me a reference point of divine blessings.

21.   Let blessings invade my life, in the name of Jesus.

22.   Let the anointing of excellence fall on me, in the name of Jesus.

23.   I disarm satan as king and authority over my prosperity, in the name of Jesus.

24.   Let harvest overtake harvest in my life, in the name of Jesus.

25.   Let harvest overtake the sower in my life, in the name of Jesus.

Course Sixteen
THE FEAR OF THE LORD

*   PRACTICAL TRAITS:
*   She fears the Lord.
*   She attributes all goodness to the Lord.
*   She is not conceited.
*   She is not vain.
*   She is not full of herself.
*   She is clothed with sobriety.

*   **THE SCRIPTURAL FOUNDATION**
      Favour is deceitful, and beauty is vain: but a woman that feareth the LORD, she shall be praised. Give her of the fruit of her hands; and let her own works praise her in the gates. Proverbs 31:30 31

*   **THE SCHOOL OF GLORIOUS WOMEN**
A student in the school of glorious women knows that outer beauty is only skin deep. She knows that beauty is deceitful and passing away. She knows that without modesty, propriety and moderation which are inner qualities, outward adornment of the body e.g. braided hair, gold, pearls, or costly apparel all amount to nothing. She knows that the beauty of a glorious godly woman is from inside out. She never loses sight of the fact that good character is the real beauty. With this at the back of her mind, she is not puffed up; rather, she is thankful to God for whatever form comeliness she is endowed with.

* STEPS TO TAKE:

1. Work on your inner qualities.
2. Pamper the flesh less and focus your attention more on spiritual things.
3. Do away with "the lust of the eyes, the lust of the flesh and the pride of life."
4. Remember that there is nothing you are, or that you have that you have not been given by God.

* PRAYER POINTS:

1. O God my Father, beautify me in my husband's eyes, in the name of Jesus.
2. Spirit of humility, possess my life by fire, in the name of Jesus.
3. Holy Ghost fire, empty me of pride, in the name of Jesus.
4. Glory of God, beautify my life, in the name of Jesus.
5. My beauty shall be an advantage, not a disadvantage, in the name of Jesus.

NOTES:

_____
_____
_____
_____
_____
_____
_____
_____
_____
_____
_____
_____
_____
_____
_____
_____
_____
_____
_____
_____
_____
_____
_____
_____
_____

Chapter

11

Prayer
Points

*Husbands, love your wives, even as
Christ also loved the church, and gave
himself for it; Eph 5:25*

SECTION ONE

GENERAL WOMEN'S DELIVERANCE PRAYERS

1. Thank God for making provision for deliverance from any form of bondage.

2. Confess your sins and those of your ancestors, especially those sins linked to evil powers.

3. I cover myself with the blood of Jesus.

4. I release myself from any inherited bondage, in the name of Jesus.

5. O Lord, send Your axe of fire to the foundation of my life and destroy every evil plantation.

6. Let the blood of Jesus flush out from my system, every inherited satanic deposit, in the name of Jesus.

7. I release myself, from the grip of any problem transferred into my life from womb, in the name of Jesus.

8. Let the blood of Jesus and the fire of the Holy Ghost, cleanse every organ in my body, in the name of Jesus.

9. I break and loose myself from every inherited evil covenant, in the name of Jesus.

10. I break and loose myself from every inherited evil curse, in the name of Jesus.

11. I vomit all evil consumption that I have been fed with as a child, in the name of Jesus.

12. I command all foundational strongmen attached to my life to be paralysed, in the name of Jesus.

13. Let any rod of the wicked rising up against my family line, be rendered impotent for my sake, in the name of Jesus.

14. I cancel the consequences of any evil local name attached to my person, in the name of Jesus.

15. Pray aggressively against the following evil foundations. Pray as follows: You *(pick the under listed one by one),* loose your hold over my life and be purged out of my foundation, in the name of Jesus.
   - destructive effect of polygamy   - evil physical design
   - parental curses   - envious rivalry
   - evil dedication   - fellowship with local idols
   - demonic incisions   - demonic marriage
   - dream pollution   - evil laying on of hands
   - demonic sacrifices   - fellowship with family idols
   - demonic initiations   - inherited infirmity
   - wrong exposure to sex - exposure to evil diviners
   - demonic blood transfusion -demonic alteration of destiny
   - fellowship with demonic consultants
   - unscriptural manner of conception

16   You evil foundational plantation, come out of my life with all your roots, in the name of Jesus.

17   I break and loose myself, from every form of demonic bewitchment, in the name of Jesus.

18   I release myself from every evil dominations and control, in the name of Jesus.

19   Let the blood of Jesus be transfused into my blood vessel, in the name of Jesus.

20   Let every gate opened to the enemy by my foundation, be closed forever with the blood of Jesus.

21   Lord Jesus, walk back into every second of my life and deliver me where I need deliverance, heal me where I need healing, transform me where I need transformation.

22   I reject, revoke and renounce my membership with any evil association, in the name of Jesus.

23   I withdraw and cancel my name from any evil register, with the blood of Jesus, in the name of Jesus.

24   I reject and renounce any evil name given to me consciously or unconsciously in any evil association, in the name of Jesus.

25   I purge myself with the blood of Jesus, of all evil foods I have eaten consciously or unconsciously in any evil association, in the name of Jesus.

26   I withdraw any part of my body and blood in custody of any evil altar, in the name of Jesus.

27   I withdraw my pictures image and inner-man, from any evil altar and coffers of evil association, in the name of Jesus.

28   I return any of the things of evil association I am consciously or unconsciously connected with, their instruments and any other property at my disposal, in the name of Jesus.

29   I hereby confess total separation from any evil association, in the name of Jesus.

30   Holy Spirit, build a wall of fire round me, that will completely make it impossible for any evil spirit to come to me again.

31   I break any covenant binding me with any evil association, in the name of Jesus.

32   I break all inherited covenants binding me with any evil association, in the name of Jesus.

33   I bind the demons attached to these covenants and cast them into the deep, in the name of Jesus.

34   I resist every attempt to return me back to any evil association with the blood of Jesus, fire, brimstone and thunder of God, in the name of Jesus.

35   I renounce and revoke all the oaths I took

consciously or unconsciously, while entering any evil association, in the name of Jesus.

36   I break and cancel every evil mark, incision, and writing placed in my spirit and body as a result of my membership of any evil association with the blood of Jesus, and purify my body, soul and spirit with the Holy Ghost fire, in the name of Jesus.

37   I break all covenants inherited from my ancestors, on the father's and mother's sides, in the name of Jesus.

38   Lord, break down every evil foundation of my life and rebuild a new one on Christ the Rock.

SECTION TWO

I SHALL NOT HABOUR EVIL SEEDS

1.   Let all contrary spiritual handwritings against me be blotted out by the power in the blood of Jesus.

2.   Thou Rock of Ages, fall upon and scatter, all the powers of the strong man assigned against my life, in the name of Jesus.

3.   Let every curse of the enemy be turned to blessings for me, in the name of Jesus.

4.   Let all evil weapons of the enemy assigned against my life be cut into pieces, in the name of Jesus.

5.   Let the excellence of dignity and power make me excel, in the name of Jesus.

129

6. Storms of failure, poverty and lack of development in my life, die! in the name of Jesus.

7. Evil prophecies of familiar spirits and hosts of darkness against my life, die! in the name of Jesus.

8. Every contrary fire set against my life, be quenched! in the name of Jesus.

9. Every good door shut against my life, be opened by fire! in the name of Jesus.

10. Let the wall of protection of my enemies fall upon them, in the name of Jesus.

11. Every evil visitor assigned against my life, fall down and die! in the name of Jesus.

12. Every power assigned to hinder my star from shining, fall down and die! in the name of Jesus.

13. Every evil work against the star of my life, die! in the name of Jesus.

14. Let the alliance of my enemies receive confusion, in the name of Jesus.

15. Let every valley of death and suffering assigned against my life turn to blessings for me, in the name of Jesus.

16. I receive freedom in all areas of life, in the name of Jesus.

17.   Any contrary handwriting against me in heaven, on earth or underneath the earth, be blotted out by the power in the blood of Jesus.

18.   All satanic lions roaring to swallow up my star, die! in the name of Jesus.

19.   Every evil stronghold behind problems in my life, be pulled down! in the name of Jesus.

20.   Let the salvation of God visit my life and set me free, in the name of Jesus.

21.   Every spiritual storm of poverty, be silenced! in the name of Jesus.

22   Let all my enemies be as chaff before the wind; and let the angels of the Lord chase them, in the name of Jesus.

23.   Every evil seed growing in my life, be uprooted by fire! in the name
of Jesus.

24.   Let the blood of Jesus, roll every Egyptian reproach away from my life, in the name of Jesus.

25   Let them be afraid and brought to confusion all who rejoice at my downfall, in the name of Jesus.

26   Let my enemies be clothed with shame and disgrace, in the name of Jesus.

27. Let the ways of the enemy be darkened and slippery, and let the angels of the Lord persecute them, in the name of Jesus.

28. Let destruction come upon my enemy unawares; and let his net that he had hid catch himself, into that very destruction let him fall, in the name of Jesus.

29 Let all the spiritual links that connect me with the spirit world be broken, in the name of Jesus.

30. My star shall rise to fall no more, in the name of Jesus.

SECTION THREE
MY GLORY, APPEAR BY FIRE!

1. Lord, let Jesus increase in my heart and in all associated with my life, in the name of Jesus.

2. Let God's sceptre of righteousness be witnessed and experienced in my life, in the name of Jesus.

3. O Lord, take Your place in my life, in my family and in all department of my life, in the name of Jesus.

4. O Lord, wake me up from deep spiritual slumber, in the name of Jesus.

5. O Lord, renew my mind, in the name of Jesus.

6. Let the command of the Lord bring light to my

eyes, and revival to my soul, in the name of Jesus.

7. Lord Jesus, walk on my waters, in the name of Jesus.

8. O Lord, deliver me and my family from the spirit of fear and inconsistency, in the name of Jesus.

9. Let the angels of God roll back every stone of limitation and bondage in my family, in the name of Jesus.

10. Let the resurrection power that raised Christ from the dead, overthrow spiritual entities that are sitting on the gates of my life, in the name of Jesus.

11. Let the mountains of oppression, ignorance and idolatry be uprooted from my family line, in the name of Jesus.

12. Let the light of Jesus expose every darkness and every den of wickedness in my family, let them be replaced with the light of Your countenance, O Lord, in the name of Jesus.

13. Let the light of God drown the walls of darkness around my life, in the name of Jesus.

14. Let the dayspring take the earth by the edges, and shake out all the wicked structures in my life, in the name of Jesus.

15.   O God arise! and shake all the foundations of idolatry and witchcraft out of my life, in the name of Jesus.

16.   Let the morning star of Christ and the brightness of His presence; consume every iota of darkness and satanic strongholds around my house, in the name of Jesus.

17.   Lord, by a strong east wind, drive away all the darkness that has surrounded my life all this while, in the name of Jesus.

18.   Let the dayspring shake the foundations of all satanic structures around my life, in the name of Jesus.

19.   Let the earth vomit out the wicked and silence the proud, in the name of Jesus.

20.   O Lord, throw into confusion, all the chariots of hell, all the distractions, and the spirits of deception that seeks to derail the progress of my life, in the name of Jesus.

21.   O Lord, grant me refuge and rest under Your wings, in the name of Jesus.

22.   O Lord, deliver me from every terror of the night and every arrow that flies by day, in the name of Jesus.

23.   O Lord, do a re-arrangement in my life and ministry, in the name of Jesus.

24. O God, illuminate my horizon, in the name of Jesus.

25. Let the rays of the powerful light of God introduce new ideas, new perceptions, new ways and methods of doing things, after the order of the word of God into my life, in the name of Jesus.

26. Let the protection of the Lord become the portion of my household, in the name of Jesus.

27. Let the Lord protect and gladden my heart, in the name of Jesus.

28. Let the Lord overthrow the stronghold of my enemies without mercy, in the name of Jesus.

29. Let my healing come quickly like the dawn, and my path shine even brighter till the full light of day, in the name of Jesus.

30. Let God arise, and let Him scatter and disband all the wicked spirits from my land, in the name of Jesus.

31. I activate the benefits of the blood of Jesus over my life, and my household, in the name of Jesus.

32. O Lord, anoint my head with Your oil, bless my water and bread to eat of the fat of this land, in the name of Jesus.

SECTION FOUR

PRAYERS FOR WISDOM

1. Thank the Lord from the bottom of your heart for what He will use this prayer programme to do in your life.

2. I reject every backward journey, in the name of Jesus.

3. I paralyse every strong man assigned to this institution, in the name of Jesus.

4. Let every agent of shame working against me be paralysed, in the name of Jesus.

5. I paralyse the activities of household wickedness over my life, in the name of Jesus.

6. I quench every strange fire emanating from evil tongues against me, in the name of Jesus.

7. Lord, give me power for maximum achievement in this place, in the name of Jesus.

8. O Lord, give me the confronting authority to achieve effortless results.

9. Lord, fill me with wisdom like an angel.

10. I break every curse of unfruitfulness placed upon my life, in the name of Jesus.

11.   I break every curse of untimely death, in the name of Jesus.

12.   Lord, fortify me with Your power.

13.   Let the counter-movement of the Holy Spirit frustrate every evil vice against me, in the name of Jesus.

14.   Father Lord, give me the tongue of the learned.

15.   Lord, make my voice the voice of peace, deliverance, power, and promotion.

16.   Lord, give me divine direction that will propel this institution to greatness through me.

17.   Every power assigned to use my family/job, etc, to torment me, be paralysed! in the name of Jesus.

18.   Lord Jesus, give me an excellent spirit.

19.   Thank God for answered prayers.

SECTION FIVE

FAVOUR AND BUSINESS BREAKTHROUGHS

1.   Thank the Lord because He alone can advance you.

2.   O Lord, bring me into favour with all those who will decide on my employment.

3. O Lord, cause a divine substitution to happen if this is what will move me ahead.

4. I reject the spirit of the tail and I claim the spirit of the head, in the name of Jesus.

5. I command all evil records planted by the devil in anyone's mind against my employment, to be shattered to pieces, in the name of Jesus.

6. O Lord, transfer, remove, or change all human agents that are bent on stopping my employment.

7. I receive the anointing to excel above my contemporaries, in the name of Jesus.

8. Lord, catapult me into greatness as You did for Daniel in the land of Babylon.

9. I bind every strong man delegated to hinder my progress, in the name of Jesus.

10. O Lord, dispatch Your angels to roll away every stumbling block to my employment.

11. I bind and render to naught, the spirit of ..... *(pick from the under listed),* in the mighty name of Jesus.
    - demonic antagonism - unprofitable questions
    - strife -confusion marginal success -mind blankness
    - wrong words - mind dullness
    - bad feet/bad luck - memory failure
    - demonic opinions against me
    - unprofitable controversies
    - evil collaborations

- demonic logic and unprofitable interviews

12. I claim the position of ...., in the mighty name of Jesus *(name the specific position being sought)*.

13. Lord, hammer my matter into the minds of those who will assist me, so that they do not suffer from a demonic memory loss.

14. I paralyse the handiwork of household enemies and envious agents in this matter, in the name of Jesus.

15. Let all the adversaries of my breakthroughs be put to shame, in the name of Jesus.

16. I claim the power to overcome and to excel amongst all competitors, in the name of Jesus.

17. Let any decision by any panel be favourable unto me, in the name of Jesus.
18. All competitors with me in this issue will find my feat unattainable, in the name of Jesus.

19. Praise the Lord for answered prayers.

SECTION SIX
EVER INCREASING WEALTH
1. O Lord, create newer and profitable opportunities for me.

2. Every strange fire ignited against my prosperity, be quenched! in the name of Jesus.

3. Let those sending my money to spiritual mortuary fall down and die, in the name of Jesus.

4. Every power scaring away my prosperity, be paralysed! in the name of Jesus.

5. Every familiar spirit sharing my money before I receive it, be bound permanently! in the name of Jesus.

6. Let every inherited design of poverty melt away by fire, in the name of Jesus.

7. Let every evil re-arrangement of prosperity be dismantled, in the name of Jesus.

8. Lead me O Lord, to my own land that flows with milk and honey.

9. Let satanic giants occupying my Promise Land fall down and die, in the name of Jesus.

10. O Lord, empower me to climb my mountain of prosperity.

11. Strong man of poverty in my life, fall down and die! in the name of Jesus.

12. Spirits of famine and hunger, my life is not your candidate, in the name of Jesus.

13. I remove my name from the book of financial embarrassment, in the name of Jesus.

14. Every power, reinforcing poverty against me, loose your hold! in the name of Jesus.

15. I release myself, from all bondage of poverty, in Jesus' name.

16. The riches of the Gentiles shall come to me, in the name of Jesus.

17. Let divine magnets of prosperity be planted in my hands, in the name of Jesus.

18. I retrieve my purse from the hand of Judas, in the name of Jesus.

19. Let there be a reverse transfer of my satanically transferred wealth, in the name of Jesus.

20. I take over the wealth of the sinner, in the name of Jesus.

21. I recover the steering wheel of my wealth from the hand of evil drivers, in the name of Jesus.

22. I refuse to lock the door of blessings against myself, in the name of Jesus

23. O Lord, revive my blessings.

24. O Lord, return my stolen blessings.

25. O Lord, send God's angels to bring me blessings.

26. O Lord, let everything that needs change in my life to bring me blessings, be changed!

SECTION SEVEN

KEY TO PROSPERITY

1. O Lord, reveal to me the key to my prosperity.

2. Every power sitting on my wealth, fall down and die! in the name of Jesus.

3. O Lord, transfer the wealth of Laban to my Jacob.
4. Let all those who hate my prosperity be put to shame, in the name of Jesus.

5. Every evil bird, swallowing my money, fall down and die! in the name of Jesus.

6. Every arrow of poverty, go back to where you came from! in the name of Jesus.

7. I bind every word spoken against my breakthroughs, in the name of Jesus.

8. Every business house, energised by satan, fold up! in the name of Jesus.

9. I destroy every clock and timetable of poverty, in the name of Jesus.

10. Every water spirit, touch not my prosperity! in the name of Jesus.

11.   Let men and women rush wealth to my doors, in the name of Jesus.

12.   I reject temporary blessings, in the name of Jesus.

13.   Every arrow of poverty, energised by polygamy, fall down and die! in the name of Jesus.

14.   Every arrow of poverty, energised by household wickedness, fall down and die! in the name of Jesus.

15.   Let power change hands in my finances, in the name of Jesus.

16.   Every serpent and scorpion of poverty, die! in the name of Jesus.

17.   I refuse to eat the bread of sorrow, and I reject the water of affliction, in the name of Jesus.

18.   Let divine explosion fall upon my breakthroughs, in the name of Jesus.

19.   The enemy will not drag my finances on the ground, in the name of Jesus.

20.   O Lord, advertise your wealth and power in my life.

21.   Let promotion meet promotion in my life, in the name of Jesus.

22.   I pursue and overtake my enemy, and I recover my wealth from him, in the name of Jesus.

23. Holy Spirit, direct my hands into prosperity, in the name of Jesus.

OTHER PUBLICATIONS BY DR. D. K. OLUKOYA

1. Be Prepared
2. Bewitchment Must Die
3. Biblical Principles Of Dream Interpretation
4. Born Great, But Tied Down
5. Breakthrough Prayers For Business Professional
6. Brokenness
7. Can God?
8. Can God Trust You?
9. Criminals In The House Of God
10. Command The Morning
11. Contending For The Kingdom
12. Dealing With Local Satanic Technology
13. Dealing With Hidden Curses
14. Dealing With Satanic Exchanges
15. Dealing With Witchcraft Barbers
16. Dealing With The Evil Powers Of Your Father's House
17. Dealing With Unprofitable Roots
18. Deliverance: God's Medicine Bottle
19. Deliverance By Fire
20. Deliverance From Limiting Powers
21. Deliverance From Spirit Husband And Spirit Wife
22. Deliverance Of The Conscience
23. Deliverance Of The Head
24. Destiny Clinic
25. Disgracing Soul Hunters
26. Destroying The Evil Umbrella

145

58. Power Against Marine Spirits
59. Power Against Spiritual Terrorists
60. Power For Explosive Success
61. Power Must Change Hands
62. Power Over Tropical Demons
63. Pray Your Way To Breakthroughs (third Edition)
64. Prayer Passport To Crush Oppression
65. Prayer Rain
66. Prayer Is The Battle
67. Prayer Strategies For Spinsters And Bachelors
68. Prayers To Kill Enchantment And Divination
69. Prayers To Move From Minimum To Maximum
70. Prayer Warfare Against 70 Mad Spirits
71. Prayers To Destroy Diseases And Infirmities
72. Praying To Destroy Satanic Road Block
73. Praying Against The Spirit Of The Valley
74. Praying To Dismantle Witchcraft
75. Principles Of Prayer
76. Provocation At The Corridor Of Breakthroughs
77. Release From Destructive Covenants
78. Revoking Evil Decrees
79. Satanic Diversion Of The Black Race
80. Silencing The Birds Of Darkness
81. Slaves Who Love Their Chains
82. Spiritual Terrorist
83. Smite The Enemy And He Will Flee
84. Spiritual Warfare And The Home
85. Star Hunters
86. Strategic Praying
87. Strategy Of Warfare Praying
88. Students In The School Of Fear
89. Symptoms Of Witchcraft Attacks
90. Technical Prayers To Disgrace Local Goliath

OTHER PUBLICATIONS IN YORUBA AND FRENCH LANGUAGES